WRITERS WORKSHOP
IN A BOOK

WRITERS WORKSHOP IN A BOOK

The Squaw Valley Community
of Writers
on the Art of Fiction

Edited by Alan Cheuse and Lisa Alvarez
Introduction by Richard Ford

CHRONICLE BOOKS
SAN FRANCISCO

Library of Congress Cataloging-in-Publication Data available.

ISBN-10: 0-8118-5821-9
ISBN-13: 978-0-8118-5821-2

Manufactured in the United States of America

Designed by Jacob T. Gardner
Typeset in Historical Fell Type Roman and Sabon

10 9 8 7 6 5 4 3 2

Chronicle Books LLC
680 Second Street
San Francisco, California 94107

www.chroniclebooks.com

To Oakley and Barbara Hall

Acknowledgments

We thank Jonathan Cohen for his careful transcribing from voice to page, Andrew Tonkovich for patient editorial assistance, Elizabeth Eshelman for her reader's eye, Emma Cheuse for her good job, and Nancy Wendt and the late Alexander Cushing and the staff of the Squaw Valley Ski Corporation for their continuing support of our creative endeavors. Thanks to Blair Fuller, and to Michael Carlisle for his good labors on our behalf.

The Community of Writers has been sustained through the years by the support of generous friends and donors, near and far, and we thank them.

The following essays have appeared in somewhat different form in the following publications: "Wrecked" in *Swing*; "'Here's Lookin' at You, Kid': A Brief History of Point of View" in the *Santa Monica Review*; "When You Write a Historical Novel" in *The Writer*; and "Angst and the Second Book" in *Publishers Weekly*. "Event and Meaning in the Scene" is adapted from Sandra Scofield's book *The Scene*

Book: A Primer for the Fiction Writer. "Making Workshops Work" is adapted from Sands Hall's book *Tools of the Writer's Craft*. "On False Starts" appeared in Lynn Freed's book *Reading, Writing, and Leaving Home: Life on the Page*.

TABLE OF CONTENTS

FOREWORD

by Alan Cheuse and Lisa Alvarez

Summer writers' conferences have blossomed wildly over the past three decades. In places where the sun shines steadily and creeks or rivers run or lakes and mountains beckon, it's difficult *not* to find a gathering of professional writers, novelists, short story writers, nonfiction writers, essayists, journalists, poets, and, here and there, playwrights and screenwriters nestled into the courtyard of a university or college or under a shady grove of trees, with attentive conference participants presenting their work for critique and hoping to be *discovered*. Or at least to acquire some new techniques, or to engage old methods, that will help improve their chances of being discovered.

The Squaw Valley Community of Writers in Northern California—as Oakley Hall, one of its cofounders, points out in his afterword—is one of the oldest in the country. As the roster of distinguished and accomplished contributors to this volume would suggest, the Community of Writers is one of the most successful and attractive conferences in the world. It also stands as one of the weeklong workshops where participants find the recognition their work deserves and where their careers kick in to overdrive—witness talented writers such as Alice Sebold, Michael Chabon, Amy Tan, and [YOUR NAME GOES HERE], among others, who have gone from workshops in the public bar at the former Olympic sports complex to a life of growing readerships and literary awards.

We hope that this collection of representative essays on various aspects of literary technique—almost all of them adapted from talks and lectures the writers have delivered to workshop participants over the years—will renew the energy and aspirations of those thousands of dedicated writers who have toiled in the workshops over the past thirty years and will charge the hopes and visions of new writers who have yet to roll into the valley, manuscripts in one hand, their hearts in the other.

INTRODUCTION
by Richard Ford

Can you teach someone to write? I'm asked that a lot—usually by Europeans who think you can't, and who think Americans are school-crazy, and that we believe anything from small engine repair to a faith in the deity can be cooked up into a syllabus and successfully imparted by tutelage with a degree at the end. These doubters—I suppose they're purists (always a rogue element in the arts)—believe that only mysterious talent, inspiration, and something else they're not entirely sure of can ever produce a real writer. "Real" is always stressed, as if Tennessee Williams and Flannery O'Connor, Larry McMurtry and Raymond Carver, were all ersatz writers who would have been genuine only if they'd just stayed home and suffered, and not gone to Iowa or Stanford; and as if anything along the way to a writer's vocation could ever free any of us from a need for talent, inspiration, and something else not quite definable.

What I usually answer to these doubters about teaching is, "Well, it all depends on what you mean by *teach*." A part of me wants to say, "No, of course you can't teach someone to write," and to dignify the question by going to its heart.

You probably *can't* teach someone to write if "teaching" means giving general instruction about how, for example, Gabriel García Márquez decides to make a stream of a dead man's blood lead out of a house and course all the way across a village to the dead man's mother's house. You can read *One Hundred Years of Solitude* right up to the moment in that miraculous novel when Márquez elects that the blood flowing will be the next thing that'll make good sense. But you can't make a syllabus topic out of exactly what went on in the author's head as he figured out what he should do. Márquez himself probably couldn't tell you. Or if he did he might misremember. Or he might just not tell you the truth. You also can't teach how Faulkner came up with the idea of *The Sound and the Fury* by (as he alleged) seeing a little girl with soiled undies crawling through a window. There really are a lot of things that live in the very genie soul of writing fiction that you can't teach at all. You just have to stand in wonder that a human being did it.

Though to be led to a point of wonder is probably pretty valuable instruction for a beginning writer, who, because of youth or inexperience, might not have recognized wonder for what it is, and might have thought it was just confusion and a blank wall. You probably *can* teach someone to recognize wonder. Stopping at a point of wonder, after all, makes us savor literature's great magic and feel exhilarated and renewed, which could encourage someone to want to produce a similar effect using a piece of writing as an instrument. That's what happened to me forty years ago.

In a sense we *are* teaching writing when we put wonder on display. It's even possible to say that any would-be writer who can't experience wonder isn't going to amount to much—which itself is worth knowing. When Flannery O'Connor was asked if writing programs and similar forums of writerly instruction discouraged young writers, she's reported to have said that they probably didn't discourage enough of them. And when I've been asked to give one piece of important advice to young writers, I've always said that they should treat the decision to write like a decision to get married: Try to talk yourself out of it if you can. And if you can't, well, then you've learned something.

For almost forty years now the Squaw Valley Community of Writers has been doing its best to expose its students to the wonder that is or can reside in excellent writing, by employing the talents, the belief, and the experience of a mostly goodwilled contingent of writer-practitioners, of whom I've been one, having first been a student there myself in the late 1960s. It's very likely that by our "teachings" we have satisfied O'Connor's dictum by discouraging more than we've encouraged. There's no reason, after all, that any generation should ever produce a *lot* of good writers. Apart from native talent always being in short supply, writing well can seem like hard work and be solitary, and plenty of people who start out thinking writing's a good idea don't want to take things that far. Life also throws impediments in the way like a wedding guest tossing rice. You get sick, divorced, go broke, turn to booze or drugs or both or worse. You get a better deal from the advertising agency or the law firm. You have a bunch of screaming kids. You die before your opus is finished. I could go on. And most people who survive these natural pitfalls—including having some talent—still turn out not to be very good writers and never will be, for some reason known only to God. And by various gentle means we writer-practitioners have accepted the challenge of explaining and sometimes even personally demonstrating this lack of worthiness, or just lack of good fortune, in workshops, in conferences, in letters, in essays, in lectures—all of which may be thought of as forms of teaching. After which these once-hopeful writer tryouts see that their dream of writing was possibly a mistake, or was at least unfairly optimistic, and can then go home to Palos Verdes or Baton Rouge happy not to have to fret about it anymore. Or else they don't do that. Or else they go home and write a wonderful novel or a story collection that proves us all wrong, proves that wonder can't be taught but also not discouraged. And then all of us who were the teachers can quietly take satisfaction that we "had a hand" in another writer's early success.

I once sat out on a sun-shot deck of an August morning, going carefully through some extraordinary pieces of narrative submitted to me by a young Amy Tan. To my credit I saw the vivid genius in these pieces. But I could see no way that they could be made into anything but vivid pieces. Perhaps the writer, I said sagely, should think of these as evidence of genuine talent, but that since they didn't "hang together," setting them aside and commencing something more obviously cohesive might be the thing to do. Don't get stuck, I said, on what are just bits of good writing and expend time trying to make them fit together when they probably won't. Amy, whose essay appears in this volume, was very appreciative and quite polite, as I remember. I was very admiring of her nascent talents, wished her well with her work, and then went on my way. When I next saw those promising pieces of vivid writing they were magically interlocked into *The Joy Luck Club*. And that's all I need to say about that display of wonderment in its struggle with the teaching arts.

But back to my point of "it depends on what you mean by *teach*." For nearly four decades *something* has been going on at the Squaw Valley Community of Writers that has worked out very well for a great, great number and variety of women and men who brought their work to the conference and experienced that work being taken seriously, read carefully, spoken of intelligently and with respect, and more often than not, made better. It happened to me, in 1970, with the careful and patient attentions of Peter Matthiessen, then a Community of Writers staff member and now my friend. And whether I or anyone would say I was *taught* by Peter or not, it's definitely the case that I and many others went home in mid-August in possession of a crucial experience we likely didn't have in July.

Exactly what that Squaw Valley experience might be deserves to be mentioned, since some of it is distilled and also elaborated upon in the essays that follow. In this volume you can learn about structuring a story or a novel (i.e., how to think about and decide what to put after what) from novelist and Community of Writers Director Emeritus Oakley Hall. You can read about point of view (by what narrative agency your story gets told—first or second person, etc.) from short story writer and novelist Alan Cheuse. You can read novelist and National Book Award winner Robert Stone on the essentialness of fiction to our very lives, and Pulitzer Prize winner Michael Chabon on novelistic failure and resurrection. Nobody—and this would please my purist European friends—is going to pronounce any hard-and-fast rules or black-letter laws about writing, since no such laws were in force when Márquez had that blood flow through town, and we "teachers" would like to encourage that brand of imaginative freedom if we can.

In these essays, just as when one is present at the Community of Writers itself, you are simply made privy to the thinking and weighing and considering done by women and men for whom this enterprise (writing) has been a lifetime vocation that's worked out well, resulting in good writing being done and literature's ends being well served. The basic idea is that for writers, who often learn things mysteriously—through the soles of our feet, by accident, by omission, from a vision glimpsed outside the normal field of vision—for these people, it's good and valuable just to be in the room when serious talk's in the air, whether it's a matter of fixing your own story's ending, or fixing someone else's, or talking about endings in general, or just helpfully talking about something entirely different, during which discussion something unexpected gets figured out and a small clarity shines through. Flannery O'Connor also used to say that to be a writer you have to be present at your work every day, whether you finally write anything or not. These essays permit you and your work to be present. And when that happens good things occasionally occur.

I know this is getting longer than it should be. Possibly one of these essayists will read it and give me some "feedback." But just one more thing. When writers take the trouble to stand up in front of strangers who would be writers if they could be, and put themselves and their own writing and their intelligence on public display, there is always one basic reason for it (though there may be other reasons, too), and that is to offer ourselves not as models or experts but as specimens—

case studies, if you please—which illuminate how writers actually conduct themselves (sometimes well, sometimes not), how rather ordinary we are, how so much of what we do are matters of perseverance, luck, accident, inspiration, wit, daring, and sometimes daring's opposite. This we do, as here, so that you who are present will understand a writing vocation a little better, and so that you will not feel discouraged—just as we were not—about literature, and can to the best of your abilities get your precious work done.

—*2006*

How to Write a Novel

by Diane Johnson

Most people don't write novels; it's a dull, contemplative, and undynamic activity, and hard to talk about. I have heard that most people in their lives think at one time or another of writing one nonetheless. I once read that, I think, 90 percent of college-educated women, at one stage or another of their lives, actually begin one. Where the men are in this I don't know, though everyone, we have heard, has at least one novel in him or her—the novel of his own life, of that great transcendent experience that has shaped him, the strange circumstances from which he sprang. If you have the least imagination, your own life will have caught it, or ought to have.

Ought—a strange peremptory word to come up so often in connection with novel writing. *You ought to write a novel*, people say to anyone with a gripping personal tale. Sometimes they say *you ought to write my novel*, my story—but I'll get to that. Peremptory suggestions of duty surround literary composition, and if it's not too far-fetched, I sometimes think we have been innately imbued with a feeling of obligation, to our family or the human race, to preserve a record of our experiences. We value testimony, we value history, we value guidance and inspiration. And we value cautionary tales.

Yet most people don't get around to writing their novel —thank heavens. It's an eccentric activity actually practiced by few. Maybe most people have the sense not to write one, for there are lots of things to be said against novel writing, and I'd like to start by mentioning a few.

Some are practical objections—it gets harder and harder to get novels, especially first novels, published, and increasingly we hear of established novelists who are dropped and can't get a new novel published. Publishers are fond of saying that all novels that should be published eventually will be, but I'm not sure I believe this. Then there is the impediment of the agent—of getting an agent, I mean—and the increasing influence of agents means that fewer and fewer unsolicited manuscripts get read, though some publishers claim to read their "slush piles" (lovely term), and of course there are examples of great best-sellers being found there.

The odds are against it.

Then, if fame and money are your objects, getting published is hardly a sure way of achieving them. Some do get these huge advances you read about, but that is hardly the rule, and the fact is that a million-dollar advance to author A restricts the funds available for poor author B—it comes out of the hides of other authors, because the giant advances seem only to be the reflex of competition among editors, and these books rarely earn back what the publishers have paid.

Anyhow, say you get a nice, respectable $100,000 advance: You will have to spend two years at least writing. That's $50,000 a year, of which $7,500 will go to the agent and then, after taxes of 30 percent, you now have around $29,000 per year. That is not the big money authors dream of.

Next, the reviewing situation gets worse and worse. There was the recent upheaval at the *New York Times*, the most influential of reviewing organs—that they were going to concentrate on best-sellers and commercial fiction and already established authors and genres—supporting the book trade, basically. Not a lot of help for that special little novel not destined to sell much, though perhaps to be acclaimed.

Suppose, though, that none of this means anything to you—you just want to write. That's the case with most of us. We don't care about fame or money; we want to communicate, we want to express, we want to write, and so we will. Yet there are still things to be said against the practice of fiction. I've had many conversations with other writers and we never can agree on whether writing is fun or torture. Obviously it's a special variety of both. If it were really torture, you wouldn't do it, and when it's going well, writing is wonderfully exhilarating.

The torture comes when you are stuck on things, your fingers seem disconnected from your brain, your entire life erupts in distracting screeches around you, and you read what you've written and it's awful. The despair produced by realizing that what you've written is terrible and that you won't be able to write another word and that your brain has gone soft is unequalled by other kinds of despair.

When things are going well, you do have the feeling of pleasure and order that always rewards the artist, and you have the added satisfaction of feeling that you've gotten away with something, that the trick you're pulling on the world is working, that the world is paying you to sit cozily in your room making up stories. The pleasure of making up stories outweighs inconvenience, financial sacrifice, and social disapproval. These things don't make you a novelist by themselves, but they make you like other novelists.

What then are novelists and fiction writers like? My impression is that writers in general, but especially fiction writers, are pleasant people. They like each other. My impression ten years ago was that women writers like each other better than male writers like them or each other, but I think that was because the class of woman writers was smaller with less range for incompatibility. Now that there are as many women writing as there are men, it is unlikely that the women will retain the sisterly feelings of a small clan. Novelists in general, I also think, are slightly suspicious of our unruly brethren the poets. Novelists, with some famous exceptions, tend to be socially cooperative, try to behave well at parties, wish to be loved, and if they have a besetting vice as a group, it is well known to be drink, with drugs somewhere in there but on the wane and in the minority. But they never, or seldom, roister in the fashion approved for poets.

I've mentioned that a novelist is an odd thing to be. Many years ago I came up with an example based on experience from the fact that you'd think twice before telling someone sitting next to you on a plane that you were a novelist. To begin with, people don't believe you. I have an explanation for this: I think it's because each person feels in himself that unwritten novel trying to get out and knows he hasn't actually sat down to let it out, hasn't sat down at the computer and done his novel, and he suspects that you haven't either. If your seatmate learns you have, he finds it irritating and reproachful. He's also equally suspicious if you are willing and if you aren't willing to listen to his novel idea. If you listen, you'll steal it, and if you don't, he's insulted that you find it dull. (Parenthetically, I think the novel someone tells you about on the airplane never gets written. Not only does that narrator discharge the energy in telling that he should use in writing, but the good story, the "I could write a novel" sort of experience, doesn't usually happen to writers, who are timid creatures in the main, endurers of plain lives. They sit at home and write novels about things that have happened to them—I think all fiction is in some sense autobiographical—but they usually have to try to make more interesting the events of a life that, unadorned by art, would be of interest only to them. One embellishes a life, life in general, and reorganizes it. One of the reasons for writing novels is surely a wish to put things in a better order.)

The person on the plane, and your relatives and friends too, are afraid you will put them in your novel, but also that you won't. My own experience in this matter is that usually people don't recognize unpleasant portraits of themselves in my novels. Vanity explains this. Sometimes they do recognize *parts* of themselves. We have a doctor friend who is noted for his far-fetched stories, and when I put him into a novel, *Persian Nights*, as a blowhard Texan, he was complimented, he said, but peeved that I had stolen the stories he would put into the novel he would someday write. Sometimes people recognize themselves or others when you haven't put them there.

The truth is that there's a sense in which nonwriters mistrust and even dislike novelists for reasons the writer herself is conscious of—because writers seem to be getting away with something, sitting around all day not working and getting paid for it, mooning, staring out windows, failing to speak when spoken to—projecting the appearance of indolence. My husband, John, the most supportive and loyal of mates and a writer himself, still is apt to come into my study and say, "Since you aren't working, how about lunch?" misled by the fact that I'm standing up reading old postcards and working nonetheless.

Anyone who's written a novel will agree that it's an awful lot of work. Just putting down all those words requires stamina—a short novel is at least some eighty thousand words. There are lots of maxims about the proportion of inspiration to perspiration needed for genius, but alas, no matter how hard you are working, some of that work will take the form of staring out the window, and that looks like not working, explain it how you will.

The final reason for people's suspicion of novelists is that novels, it is well known, are lies. Poems are true cries from the soul, but fiction is not truth: "story" is a euphemism for "fib." So you are a professional liar, and I think there is more latent disapproval of this than most people would care to admit. Recently I was quite hurt when my friend Mary Blume, herself a writer but not of fiction, suggested I be the one to make an excuse about an event we didn't want to go to. "You're the best liar in Paris," she said, meaning it as a great compliment. Of course, since I think of myself as an utterly truthful, straightforward person, I was horrified at this characterization, but I came to see that we novelists are liars by profession, and it isn't surprising if our personal rectitude gets overlooked.

These are all the disadvantages of writing fiction. You won't pay attention to them, you want to write a novel; what happens to you now?

You have an urgent novel and you want to write it. First you have to plan it. What will happen in it? Who will tell it? And where will it take place? Three elementary concerns. Every novel is a series of choices. By making one kind of choice—about the plot, or characters, or how it shall be told—you rule out all others. These choices are conscious, the dictates of craft, and they are unconscious, the dictates of your nature. I think the latter are more determining than we realize. You choose this word instead of that, you make something happen in the afternoon instead of evening, you make the character ride a bus instead of going in a cab. Easy enough. Some of the choices will affect the whole novel. Will the novel be told in the first person, by an I, or will he or she tell the story, and, if so, what is the name of that character and what will be his relation to the events of the story? This is the spot I find myself in at the moment, beginning a novel, and thus in the throes of the very process I am assigned to talk about. I'm trying to write a spy story set in Morocco. It's a first-person tale and the heroine is a CIA agent. I'm constantly rethinking those choices, mined with doubts on the one hand, plunging ahead on the other.

Small and large choices. I, the narrator, am wearing a blue, no, a green dress . . . when you're finished with all these choices, the result, like it or not, resembles a novel you, not someone else, would write. You had hoped, this time, to escape the imperatives of your nature, but you haven't. I always set myself out a scheme that I hope will escape confirming a phrase I read once about my novels—"her usual blend of malaise and mayhem"—but I always seem to end up with something like that. My novel *Le Divorce* was meant to escape in the direction of tender romantic comedy, but lo—there was a body in the garbage can and a hostage siege and a suicide attempt . . .

What your novel will be about, then, is decided in some mysterious way by the imperatives of your nature, by your experience, by your feeling that something should be done or said about something—we are all didactic underneath. The novel's shape, the details of it, will issue from the choices. You will decide on the characters: they will be improved or slandered versions of people you know, with blond curls put on the dark, straight-haired originals, and the ones you dislike made bald or fat, or, if you are very sly, you make the hero bald. You keep in mind the overall effect of baldness in our society and work with or against that stereotype, for you must know everything you can about the literary tradition in which you are working.

Where will your novel be set? Until we moved to France, all my novels had been set in California, with the exception of one in Persia when we were there. I think that there are still perils to setting novels in California. In the minds of people elsewhere, it seems there is a genre called the "California novel" that signals to the reader the presence of dope, violence, strange philosophies, laid-backness, and starlets. My novels set in California had those ingredients. But what I have noticed is that people elsewhere don't feel that these ingredients have any universality or power to reflect the constants of human nature or the qualities of American life. California is just too weird. People are wrong, as they will find out when developments mentioned in California novels begin to apply to their lives ten years later. Meantime you work at a disadvantage. Those of you who are employed at a university should be warned off that as a setting for many of the same reasons.

Who will tell the story? This is the thing vexing me at the moment, though I have settled on a first-person narrator. And she is a woman—here I fly in the face of some pitfalls. I continue to be fascinated with the way readers take what a female first-person narrator says with a grain of salt. There is almost no tradition of reliable woman narrators; they are thought to be emotional, neurotic, subjective, victims—and sometimes that's what the narrative requires. But in a political novel, or something meant to have archetypal mythic significance, be warned.

Now, let's say you know who's in your novel and where it happens, and how it's told, and how, generally, it's going to end, or at least the tone of the ending. I, like everyone, have trouble with endings because they have an unfair weight. Many a wonderful novel has been turned on by its disappointed reader. A good example is Susanna Moore's *In the Cut*, if anyone's read that gripping novel spoiled by its ending; a kind of wild, desperate young woman understands that she's being stalked, she puts herself in ever and ever more dangerous situations—how is she going to get out? The suspense is skillfully managed, then the ending . . . "Whoops, he got me, I'm dead!" All along she's been speaking from beyond the grave or something. How to chart the course of a novel so as to avoid such a wreck at the end?

When I was teaching creative writing at the University of California at Davis, I would always nag my class about making outlines. I am committed to them, though I've come to see that *outline* is not a good word; it seems too over-determined and writer's manual–ish. *Model* or *diagram* might be better words; any device for enabling you to lay the parts out, like the hotels on a Monopoly board, and somehow grasp the form of your undertaking, the order of events, the interchangeability of the parts—a way of visualizing a work before it begins and anticipating some of the problems before you have written them deeply into the organic structure of the novel, making it harder to change. Every novelist must have what his readers can never have, a liberated sense of the complete arbitrariness of the parts of his fiction. Most people understand that you can push a button and change George to Henry. Editors and publishers also understand that you can let Maureen live or kill her off, or get Charles and Annette into bed together as early as chapter two. Contrary to popular impression, by the way, in my experience they never suggest more sex—such explicit instructions would be easier than the expressions of nebulous discontent with which publishers just want you to make your novel better.

Even when you've answered all the technical questions, you will still want to devise some trick for getting yourself to sit down and write. Some writers are almost as famous for their tricks as for their works—unfairly in the case of Trollope, a great novelist who doomed himself to being thought of for too long as a kind of hack by confessing in his memoirs that if he finished a novel during his five-in-the-morning stint before his day job, he would not take the morning off; he'd begin another.

You don't want to underemphasize the importance of ritual (neither should it rule) nor of other psychic demands, for, while you mustn't let them control the situation, you can't do without them. The unconscious plays a huge part in literary composition; occasionally, when you're waking up or falling asleep, you can catch it at work. I know that the more I write, the more I respect the unconscious artistic work that goes on within the writer, and I wish I knew how to keep that inner being fed and happy and at work. This sense of one's self as a mysterious creature needing some pampering underlies the occasional erratic and demanding nature of writers that other people find so irritating. It will be up to you to keep your sense of yourself as a mysterious vessel mostly unnoticed by others.

A supportive friend or two is essential—not those prone to empty praise, to be sure, but good readers. You may go through a few friends by trial and error until you find one that delivers the right mixture of understanding and suggestion. Mindless praise, as from one's spouse or mother, is really not a help.

One objection I always have to workshops is "I really like this and that," praise instead of analysis of how things can be made better, and everything *can* be made better. I caution students from basking in the praise they will receive from most people, no matter how lame the story, because for most people, any story at all is miraculous, and you are the cleverest person on earth to be able to do it. But beware also of the wrong sort of critic, who will say, "That's great, but she could be older, and then you could set the story in Minneapolis . . ." and go on to propose that you in effect write his story.

Who, where, what, when are questions to answer before you start writing. All this is not to beg but only to defer the hardest question of all: what is my novel about? It is often a difficult question to answer at the beginning of the process, when these other technical issues are the focus. Yet the answer to it must be faced at least by the novelist. If the answer is conditions faced by crews on tramp steamers in the 1930s, fine, why not? If it's how I have suffered a mean family, that's harder. It may be better consciously to frame that answer in a more positive way. How I overcame a tough childhood; better, how tough childhoods can be overcome. What a novel is about is ultimately what people will notice about it, and also what has to keep you yourself interested during the time of its composition. And you may not know the answer entirely until you've finished, but the knowledge will then help you in your revisions. Try to think of revision as fun.

Now, pile up your blank white paper, and off you go.

—2004

WRECKED

by Michael Chabon

In 1987, in the final stages of work on my first novel, *The Mysteries of Pittsburgh*, I came upon a little picture that nearly ruined my life. It was a reproduction of an aerial painting of Washington, D.C., by the architectural visionary Léon Krier—a tiny prospect of blue water, white avenues, green promenades, glimpsed from a tantalizing distance, unattainable, ever-receding. My reaction to this picture was strange: my heart began to pound, the hair on the back of my neck stood up, and I felt a sadness come over me, a powerful sense of loss, which I began at once to probe and develop, thinking that in an attempt to explain the inexplicable ache this little picture caused in my chest there might lie the matter of a second novel. I didn't know that what I was feeling was a prefigurative pang of mourning for the next five years of my creative life.

I felt I had stumbled across a kind of treasure map to the barnacle-encrusted wreck of something true and important sunk deep inside of me, and I decided to try to bring it up and expose it to the light. Five years and some fifteen hundred pages later I was still trolling the murky waters of the Innermost Sea, in search of that fabled wreck, which by then I was calling *Fountain City*. In that time, I had found fantastic, shattered hulks and ruins down there, helmets and rimy flatware, chests of moldering silk, astrolabes, the skeletons of men and horses, but nothing that I felt could honestly be considered treasure. And when, at the end of 1992, with the help of my editor, Doug Stumpf, I tried one last time to hoist the whole rotten caravel to the surface, it all just fell apart.

In the aftermath of this debacle, though I kept it to myself, I felt bewildered, depressed, and, to be honest, terrified. I was not accustomed to failure, nor to the bathyspheric pressures that weigh on a second novel, particularly when the first has met with any kind of success. The pressure I felt while writing *The Mysteries of Pittsburgh* had been entirely different in nature. I'd had no readers then, no book contract, no reputation, nothing but an MFA thesis to be written and a vague sense that in stringing together the seven thousand sentences of that thesis I was forging an identity for myself, in the world, as a novelist—or else failing abjectly to do so. It never occurred to me that if *Mysteries* didn't pan out I would be able to try again; I attempted to put into that book everything I had ever learned or felt, and to use every single word I knew. This purely internal pressure—to become, once and for all, a writer—was thrilling, astringent, it whetted the appetite; and I could feel myself succeeding in my ambition, or so I thought, with each new chapter I wrote. Most of the time the work, however slow or difficult, was also a hell of a lot of fun.

Writing *Fountain City*, on the other hand, was mostly no fun at all. Where *Mysteries* had been a kind of Drake's voyage, a wild jaunt in a trim ship to make marvelous discoveries and conduct raucous pirate raids on the great ports of American literature, *Fountain City* was more like the journey of Lewis and Clark, a long, often dismal tramp through a vast terrain, in pursuit of a grand but fundamentally mistaken prize. Mosquitoes, sweltering heat, grave doubts, flawed maps—and, in my case, no Pacific Ocean at the end.

What was it about? This, unfortunately, is what I could never quite figure out: the great River of the West my large, well-equipped expedition never managed to find. It was a novel about utopian dreamers, ecological activists, an Israeli spy, a gargantuan Florida real estate deal, the education of an architect, the perfect baseball park, Paris, French cooking, and the crazy and ongoing dream of rebuilding the Great Temple in Jerusalem. It was about loss—lost paradises, lost cities, the loss of the Temple, the loss of a brother to AIDS, and the concomitant dream of Restoration or Rebuilding. It was also, naturally, a love story, an account of a love affair between a young American and a Parisian woman ten years his senior. The action was divided between Paris and the fictitious town of Fountain City, Florida. But I could never get those two halves to stick together convincingly, and I knew just enough about most of the above-mentioned subjects to be able to persuade the reader that they didn't all belong in the same book together.

So, at the beginning of 1993, after sixty-two months of more or less steady work and four drafts, each longer than the previous one, I dumped it. I didn't tell anyone, not even my wife, Ayelet, though unwittingly she provided the impetus that led me to leave that long-ago ache of architectural longing forever unexplained. We were living in San Francisco at the time, where Ayelet, a lawyer, was working as a clerk for a federal judge. She was due to take the California bar exam in July of that year, but one morning in January she announced that she didn't want to wait that long, and that, if I had no objection, she planned to register for the exam that was being given at the end of February—six weeks away. She felt she could be ready by then.

This came at the absolute lowest point in my years of work on *Fountain City*. Every night I went down to my computer in the room under our house on Twenty-ninth Street and sat for hours, staring at the monitor, dreaming about all the other wonderful books I could have written in the last five years. On the day my wife told me she was going to be largely unavailable for the next six weeks, I went down to my office and found myself, inexplicably, imagining a scene. A straight-laced, troubled young man with a tendency toward melodrama was standing on a backyard lawn, at night, holding a tiny winking derringer to his temple, while, on the porch of the nearby house, a shaggy, pot-smoking, much older man, who had far more reason to want to die, watched him, and tried to decide if what he was seeing was real or not. That was all I had, and yet it was so much more than I had started *Fountain City* with. I opened a new file and called it X. I started to write, and quickly found the voice of that shaggy old watcher in the shadows.

The first fifty pages wrote themselves in a matter of days. I said nothing to Ayelet or anyone else, but privately I had decided that I would take these six weeks of relative solitude and give this new thing, still in a file called X, a chance to grow. If nothing came of it, I would go back to *Fountain City*, having wasted only a month and a half. What was a month and a half out of five years?

The new book seemed to want to take place in Pittsburgh, and thus, in my basement room, I returned to the true fountain city, the mysterious source of so many of my ideas. I didn't stop to think about what I was doing, whom it would interest, what my publisher and the critics would think of it, and, sweetest of all, I didn't give a single thought to what I was trying to say. I just wrote. I had characters. I had their story to tell. And, most important of all, I had the voice to tell it with. Six weeks later, after Ayelet had taken the bar exam, I took a deep breath and told her that while in all that time I'd done nothing to solve the problems of *Fountain City*, I did have one hundred and seventeen pages of a novel called *Wonder Boys*. She paled, and then gave me her blessing. At the end of May, when she learned that she had passed the exam, I was two-thirds of the way finished with the first draft.

The hardest part of writing a novel is the contemplation of the distance to the end, and the hardest part of those five years I gave to *Fountain City* was that every time I contemplated that distance, it was never any shorter, or, rather, no matter how close I came to it, I could never seem to arrive. There is no joy like the joy of finishing. "Harry finished the model of Fountain Field," I wrote of my apprentice architect in *Fountain City*, who is assigned to the building of a presentation model for a proposed ballpark, with a week to spare, at three o'clock in the morning.

> He took off his shirt and whirled it over his head like
> a lariat, assumed a soul-transporting Jackie Wilson fal-
> setto, and switched from plain old skipping to the cool
> cool jerk. He jerked past closed office doors, slap, slap,
> slapping them with his bullwhip shirt. He cool-jerked

into the foyer, made a reckless circuit of the reception-
ist's desk, banked steeply, and then set off across the
drawing room once more. He played the drum solo
from "Wipeout" on the drafting tables.

I wrote that passage somewhere in the middle of the
fourth year of that expedition, and you can see how thirsty
I was. It almost makes me feel sorry for myself, this pathetic
attempt to give myself a kind of false taste, four years in, of
the sweet nectar of completion. But then I remind myself that
if only I'd had more courage, I would have dumped *Fountain City* years before I ever reached this lamentable state. I
would not have given a thought to the money I had already
accepted, to the second-novel-savaging critics I imagined I
was going to have to face, to the readers, however few or
many of them there might be, who were expecting me to
take them someplace worth going.

Six weeks after Ayelet passed the bar, I sent the completed manuscript of a decent first draft of *Wonder Boys*
to Mary Evans, my agent. Then I called her up and told her
that I had finally finished my second novel. She said she was
pleased, but I thought I could hear a faint note of weariness
or wariness enter her voice at the thought of reading yet
another interminable draft of *Fountain City*.

"There's just one thing you probably should know," I
told her, and then, as I started to cool-jerk my way across
my living room, I gave her the welcome news.

—*1996*

THE RECONQUEST OF REALITY

by Robert Stone

In the days when Tom Wolfe was still insisting that the novel had been replaced by his parajournalism, before the form made its amazing surprise comeback (!) with the publication of *The Bonfire of the Vanities*, a kind of Protestant sensibility prevailed. The priestcraft of fictionizers was to be dispensed with. Each reader would approach revelation directly, and reality, like scripture, would be henceforth available to any believer. Assisted by the eloquence and insight of the preacher/parajournalist, readers would tackle the thing itself. The childish process of sheer invention had been obviated, so it was held. Truth, the real, was superior to nontruth, the unreal, the fictive. It was a principle of ontology.

During the 1960s, a decade awash in renaissances and reformations, this looked like progress. Possibility ran rampant; everything could be had any which way. Thus we could have, for example, Leonard Bernstein's shindig for the Black Panther Party rendered with the brio of good fiction and the informational quality of the morning paper. A double bonus was offered here. The subjective descriptions and the play of dialogue served to characterize each person definitively. Bernstein and his guests were available to the reader with the authority and intimacy of omniscient narration; at the same time it was news—it had all actually happened. The reader could be a fly on the wall.

Beneath the flourishes, Tom Wolfe writes very sound demotic prose, and his hyper-conscious, media-madness style has been honored by the homage of a thousand imitators. It's still satisfying, though, to have, in the form of his own novels, an implicit concession to the irreplaceability of fiction.

Everyone who has ever tried to convey a situation of any complexity knows how hard it is to keep facts from getting in the way of truth. Some very good reporters have written some very fancy prevarications trying. There is always a temptation in journalism to enhance reality, lest the big picture get lost, and to keep it all simple for the readers. And for each enhancement of commission there have been twenty of omission. The perpetrators have usually seen themselves in the service of some higher honesty, something finer than the soulless enumeration of statistics or the transcription of mere anecdotes. And if the cause of truth was also, somehow, humanity's cause—all the more reason not to be a philistine about it, enslaved to boring details. But at a certain point, honorable lies told in the name of the big picture corrupt. Journalists who suppress their scruples in this regard have begun to despise their own profession and end by being simply unscrupulous journalists.

The traditional way of preserving truth from the hickory-dickory-dock distractions of gross phenomenology is by inventing. In the world of fiction, the author is king, the dispenser of doom and grace, the world's foremost authority on anything within the confines of his fiction. But why should one person pay attention to the vain imaginings of another? What use is it?

The fact is that many people don't read fiction. (Most people in the United States don't read books at all.) Those who do find in it special satisfactions available nowhere else. The sensation of being seduced by a fiction is very satisfying and can be surprisingly intense. Most literate people can remember being possessed by a novel during adolescence. At fifteen, I dropped out of school for a few days to read *Look Homeward, Angel*.

In later life most of us become less easily pleased, but those fires of the heart burn on under the snow. Good fiction stirs them, and the best illuminates our inner world for a moment, connecting the sum of our experience with the child we have outgrown.

The child in us loves a good story, so the pleasure principle is always the bottom line. No work is profound enough or sincere enough to overcome its failure to entertain. Boredom is a fearful monster that stalks a writer's every inky move. Writers, who spend more time than most people trying to stay awake in quiet rooms, live in dread of it.

(The scene is a writer's study, shabby, drafty but tax-deductible. The writer is rereading the last hundred pages of his work in progress. For the past fifty or so, a kind of slow terror has been rising in his breast. All these pages had seemed necessary. They contain many good things. Ironies. Insights. And yet they seem to have a certain ineffable unsatisfactoriness. There is a word to describe this quality, the writer thinks, a horrible word. The B word. He begins to strike his high forehead with a sweaty palm.)

Though we cannot do without a good story, discriminating readers eventually require something more. Any wine can make you drunk, but there is more to drinking. Serious pleasures are best. So, once the requirement of lively narrative has been met, readers expect a few higher satisfactions. The short story and the novel developed in the Western world for certain historical reasons; its readers brought to their reading certain cultural assumptions. One, which goes back to the Old Testament, was that human life had an underlying significance, even a kind of purpose. There was a feeling that the life of man was somehow more than the meaningless play of plastic forms, all illusion. Thus the events of a human life could be examined in the name of moral speculation.

I once saw a piece of lavatory graffiti I think I'll spend the rest of life pondering. "There are no metaphors," some malcontent had written. Carried to its ultimate reduction, that assertion means that no word or act can represent anything more than itself. A world without metaphor is a hermetic nightmare, utterly incomprehensible, without the possibility of humor or insight. Everything would happen once. No individual or event could be interpreted in the light of another.

There are metaphors, though. Language exists, though its connection to reality is an ongoing open question. Literature exists. We are able to entertain narratives about other people's lives, even imaginary people's lives, and recognize elements familiar to us from our own hopes, fears, and dreams. Past lives, imaginary lives, are seen to contain messages for us, metaphorically speaking. Our understanding may draw upon them. This is the importance of fiction, that it offers meaning.

To see fiction at work in the process of signifying, consider the joke. A joke is a very simple form of fiction and one easily judged on its merits. A joke is funny or it's not. You get it or you don't. You can only get it; it can only be funny to the degree that you recognize in it something you already know. This process of recognizing ourselves in stories about other people is the beginning of all wisdom. As soon as we understand that we may draw meaning from other lives, we begin to wonder if life itself may not have an underlying meaning. It's a congenial notion. Most people suffer and would very much like it if their suffering meant something.

The Western Bible assumes that human action matters, matters even on a cosmic scale. In its view of the universe, life is not an illusion, nor does the universe consist of endless cycles eternally replaying dreams. Its God, unlike many, is directly concerned with humanity. So our ancestors examined the strange stories in the Bible for their meaning, their message. They felt certain that every story was intended as a lesson and guide. Similarly they examined Homer's stories and Plutarch's lives. The work that survives, survives only to the degree that it remains relevant, the degree to which it contains people and situations we recognize.

The element of recognition is vital. It is in the name of recognition that art conducts its shadow-dance with reality. E. H. Gombrich has an essay called "The Conquest of Reality" in his history of Western art. In it he evokes the astonished reaction of contemporaries when Masaccio's *Holy Trinity with the Virgin, St. John, and Donors* was unveiled in the Church of Santa Maria Novella in Florence in 1427. It was one of the first paintings employing the laws of perspective, then recently discovered by the Florentine architect Brunelleschi.

Before Brunelleschi, artists had ways of imparting a sense of physical depth to their work, but no one had discovered the mathematical laws by which objects diminish in size as they recede into the background. The now-ordinary trick of having an avenue of trees lead back into the picture until it seems to disappear at the horizon was then outside the painter's repertoire.

Masaccio's painting electrified those present. Today it can be seen as austere and moving. Beauty aside, it appears a conventional enough religious piece to the modern eye. The two donors kneel at either side of an arch beneath which, deeper into the wall painting, the Crucifixion is taking place. Mary and John stand under the arch at the foot of the cross. Behind them appears to be a vast chapel in the classical style then being revived by Brunelleschi. Today we can only imagine what its impact must have been.

The Florentine artists of the early fifteenth century actually changed human perception. The world before Brunelleschi was, in a certain sense, forever lost. The crowd in Santa Maria Novella was recognizing a rendering of reality such as had never been seen before.

Before then, art had sought only to restore the standards of classical times, which were imagined as impossibly high. But after Brunelleschi, more or less, art would forever stalk reality, continually seeking new techniques to capture it, to "get it right." One major criterion of art would henceforth be its verisimilitude.

The question is complicated somewhat by the fact that notions of reality change from one age to another. Present-day biblical fundamentalism, for example, is a product of the age of reason. Medieval religion flourished in a world that had quite different notions of phenomenology than ours. Its distinction between existing things and their symbolic expression is obscure and not readily available to the twentieth-century mind. Modern religious people who insist on the literal truth of Bible stories are dealing in categories unknown to the church fathers.

To what degree can literature capture the nature of things? To no greater extent than language can. Language's relationship to reality is one of the oldest questions of philosophy. The confusion between the two is an ancient fallacy; different schools of thought have been accusing each other of it since Plato's time. Today anti-Marxists attack the idea of the dialectic, that great philosophical juggernaut of German romanticism, for what they see as its naive reification of verbal logic. All the certainties of the nineteenth century seem to be evaporating, leaving us as perplexed as when we came in. We're also having the opportunity to see the degree to which state philosophies depend on the economy and military of the state that professes them.

For a long time now, writers have been trying to find some literary equivalent of Brunelleschi's laws of composition. Onomatopoeia, blank verse, naturalism, the stream of consciousness, even New Journalism, all represent a sort of Faustian struggle on the part of literature to break through the veil of language. The pursuit of the real by writers can be as grimly obsessive as Ahab's pursuit of the whale. "Strike through the mask," Ahab said to Starbuck. Norman Mailer has described fiction as "an assault on reality."

Adam is supposed to have named all the creatures of the garden in order to assert his dominion over them. Language is a way of rationalizing life, subjecting the chaos around us to the control of grammar and reason. Fiction carries this process one step further by suggesting a moral relationship between people and things as they are. Those who assert that good fiction can work its way free of moral valences are mistaken. From the most simplistic narrative with its good guys and bad guys to the most decadent and arcane poetry, wherever fiction exists, judgment is in progress. It's inescapable, built into the language, into the grammar.

Artistic attempts to close on reality flourished about the time that traditional morality, grounded in religious belief, began to be critically examined. Nietzsche lived between 1844 and 1900, the half-century during which God was proclaimed to be dead and the seeds of modernism were planted in every medium.

On one hand, art was pursuing life, trying to break out of its constraining artifice. On the other, post-Christian ideologues were trying to replace God with art. For this finally is what the mass movements of the twentieth century represented. Both the left and the right were powered by German romanticism, which became the prevailing aesthetic of the totalitarian state. The worldview of the Nazis and Communists is more like grand opera than like anything human beings could actually live out without a mixture of criminality and pretense.

If truth is beauty and beauty truth and this is all we need to know, then art and science should enable us to cope with anything. In practice they fall short of human desires. We have no sure way of telling whether our hunger for transcendence is a weakness for false gods or a message from the numinous. But truth is beauty, no doubt about it.

Art is the main process through which we achieve a consensus about how it is with us. Only art can remove a moment from the whirl of events and place it before our scrutiny. It is the place where imagination meets the greater world and each acts upon the other.

Just as an artistic cliché is the corpse of an insight, so moral clichés are the remains of moral observation, morality reduced to moralizing. Artistic kitsch is always moral kitsch. On this mysterious and perhaps even metaphysical process art rests. It has to do with nothing being free. Lies, prettifications, banalities are not just dissatisfying, they are actually wrong.

Consider what Joseph Conrad has to say about the art of fiction in his preface to *The Nigger of the "Narcissus"*:

> To snatch in a moment of courage, from the remorseless rush of time, a passing phase of life, is only the beginning of the task. The task approached in tenderness and faith is to hold up unquestioningly and without fear the rescued fragment before all eyes in the light of a sincere mood. It is to show its vibration, its color, its form, and through its movement, its form, and its color, reveal the substance of its truth—disclose its inspiring secret: the stress and passion within the core of each convincing moment. In a single-minded attempt of that kind, if one be deserving and fortunate, one may perchance attain to such clearness of sincerity that at last the presented vision of regret or pity, of terror or mirth, shall awaken in the heart of the beholders that feeling of unavoidable solidarity;

of the solidarity in mysterious origin, in toil, in joy, in hope, in uncertain fate, which binds men to each other and all mankind to the visible world.

No one has put the case for fiction more eloquently than this master of the novel. His words remind us how good fiction brings forth some of the best in us, writer and reader alike.

—*1994*

Structure

by Oakley Hall

Kipling said, "There are nine and sixty ways of constructing tribal lays, and every single one of them is right." But how do you decide which structure is right for your novel?

The structure should be the most effective presentation of a novel's treasures. It is certainly involved with plot, and with character, although as we know each of these partakes of the other. What is plot but the presentation of character? What is character but plot personified?

Story is a narrative arranged in chronological order. Plot is story with causal or motivational elements. The prince saved the princess from the tower, and married her, is a story. The prince saved the princess from the tower, and then married her against the king's command, is a plot.

This tale could be narrated in first-person point of view, in which case it is presumed to be retrospective—the prince explaining to his children, say, why he and his wife live in Cleveland, Ohio, instead of the royal palace in Graustark. In this case the author will probably choose to develop his narrative beginning at a point close to the climax, flashing back to bring the action up to that point, and finishing from there. A kind of reverse structure.

If the narrative is presented in third-person or omniscient point of view, it is presumed to be taking place before the reader's eyes. The author will then probably choose to tell the story chronologically, Point A to Point Z, forwardly.

These, to begin with, are different structures.

Let's look at some exotic structures:

Thaïs, by Anatole France, has the structure of a letter *X*. The two chief characters are Paphnuce the ascetic and Thaïs the courtesan. Paphnuce lives as a hermit in the desert, where he is saved and content. Thaïs lives a life of sin in Alexandria. It is Paphnuce's duty to save her. They meet, he succeeds, and she goes into a nunnery and gains salvation. However, because he has met her, lust has entered his soul and he is damned. His line is a descending one, from salvation to damnation, hers ascending from damnation to salvation.

A similar *X* structure is also obtained in Henry James's *The Ambassadors*, in which Strether's and Chad's stories take the *X* courses.

This is related to the double structure that John Fowles employed in *The French Lieutenant's Woman*, and which was much used in Elizabethan drama: there is a main plot featuring noble and tragic characters who speak in verse, and a secondary plot with characters of a lower social order, usually comic, who speak in prose. The BBC miniseries *Upstairs, Downstairs* made use of this structure.

Raymond Chandler employed high-life/low-life plots as the structure of many of his mysteries, with the culmination occurring at the point where the two plots intersect. Thus, in *Farewell, My Lovely*, the revelation that the stripper Velma has become the high-toned socialite Mrs. Grayle.

The structure of Ross Macdonald's mystery novels is often Oedipal, which is not a mother-son reference but implies a messenger arriving out of the past with a dire message. Some open-ended horror in the past must be resolved before the present crime can be addressed. P. D. James often uses a similar construct in her massive mystery novels, where each of the suspects is tainted with some guilty circumstance in the past that may or may not pertain to the present crime.

Sara Paretsky's crime novel *Blood Shot* employs both an Oedipal plot and the high-life/low-life connection. Her detective, V. I. Warshawski, is a hard-boiled Chicago private eye, whose area of expertise is Chicago politics, from the highest levels to the lowest.

Warshawski returns to her native South Chicago for a reunion of a high school girls' basketball team. There she receives two commissions, one from a young woman who was her admirer as a girl—to search for the young woman's lost father. The other is to discover why the local alderman has come out against a project that would seem to be of great benefit to South Chicago.

The former is the low-life plot; the latter takes Warshawski into high-level Chicago politics. Early in the novel a clever reader may be able to identify the erring alderman as the disappeared father, who is also involved in the Oedipal plot—a reeking injustice of long ago that must be solved and brought to bear on the present.

Historical novels are also concerned with high-life and low-life connections. The attitudes and loyalties of the shepherd as well as those of Oedipus must be considered, Sally Hemings's as well as Thomas Jefferson's.

Sir Walter Scott's protagonists are usually neutral in politics, which allows the author access to the opposing camps. In *Ivanhoe*, the eponymous character is an aristocratic adherent of compromise between the Saxons and their Norman conquerors. Richard Coeur de Lion is also such a (Norman) moderate. Ivanhoe's father is an uncompromising Saxon who must be brought to compromise, along with the Saxon serfs, the low-life elements, who must also learn to compromise.

The Great Gatsby is a very short novel, about fifty thousand words. The structure is simple, nine chapters like building blocks. In the fifth chapter, the center of the novel, Gatsby meets Daisy Buchanan again after many years. The seventh chapter is the climax. Each chapter consists of one or more dramatic scenes, separated by passages of first-person narration. This scenic method is one Fitzgerald learned from Henry James, and Daisy Buchanan is named for James's Daisy Miller.

Hemingway's *The Sun Also Rises*, a somewhat longer novel, has a three-act structure: situation, complication, resolution. The novel is divided into three books, like acts. Book One sets up the situation and relationships. Brett, who is to marry Mike, tells her old lover, Jake, that she will never see him again because she is straightening out her messy life. Book Two takes the cast to the fiesta in Pamplona, where relationships are intertwined and complicated. It ends with Brett running off with the young bullfighter, Romero, after his triumph in the bullring, complicating rather than straightening out her life, and endangering Romero's career.

Book Three has Jake bailing Brett out of a hotel in Madrid. She has sent Romero away, proud of herself for not being "that kind of bitch," and asserting that she and Jake could have been happy together if it had not been for his war wound. To which Jake replies, "Isn't it pretty to think so?"

In the three-act structure, the first- and second-act curtains mark the major reversals or recognitions of the plot. The first-act curtain denotes the end of the movement establishing the characters and the situation, galvanizing or reversing it. The second-act curtain performs the same function at the climax of the movement of complication and confrontation, in preparation for the final movement of resolution. In opera, the second-act climax is often a so-called avalanche curtain, which thunders down on the sustained high note of the tenor's great aria at the opera's most dramatic moment.

At the first-act curtain of *The Sun Also Rises*, Brett decides to change the destructive course of her life. The second-act curtain reverses this, for she is off on a destructive bender again.

A reversal is also a sought-after object (or an abstraction in the case of Brett's resolution) snatched away just when it is thought to be safely in hand. For instance, the black bird in *The Maltese Falcon*.

The Maltese falcon is a perfect example of a MacGuffin, a Hollywood term for the sought-after object.

A recognition would be the discovery that the sought-after bird, the MacGuffin, is not made of gold and jewels, but of lead.

Thus in *Oedipus Rex* the messenger who has come to cheer up Oedipus and free him from worries about his mother instead reveals who Oedipus really is. Instead of damping his worries, the messenger opens the door on horror. It is a reversal.

A recognition, as the name indicates, is a change from ignorance to knowledge. Usually it produces a reversal.

A three-act structure built upon two reversals can be very useful in a short novel. Certainly this can be expanded to a four- or five-act structure.

Gustav Freytag, a student of the five-act German dramas of the nineteenth century, devised what is called the Freytag Pyramid, a five-act structure.

This pyramid rises from SITUATION (i.e., relationships, compulsions, oppositions, conflict, predicament, instability) through COMPLICATION (i.e., deepening of oppositions, heightening of conflict, intensification of tension) to the CLIMAX (i.e., revelation, recognition), then descending through DENOUEMENT (i.e., reappraisal, showdown) to RESOLUTION (i.e., stability with change).

In other words, begin with the characters in conflict with each other or with some outside force. The conflicts intensify and complicate, in the rising action, to a point of overload, the crisis. Out of the crisis comes the showdown, where old relationships and patterns of behavior are demolished, and new ones revealed.

In *The Wizard of Oz*, Dorothy departs from Kansas for Oz. She returns from Oz to Kansas much changed by her experiences.

This from T. S. Eliot's "Little Gidding":

We shall not cease from exploration
And the end of our exploring
Will be to arrive where we started
And know the place for the first time.

In Henry James's *The Wings of the Dove*, Merton Densher and Kate Croy are in love, but Densher is too poor to marry a young woman of Kate's social position. Enter Milly Theale, a millionairess who is terminally ill. The lovers contrive for Milly to fall in love with Densher. They will marry, Milly will die, leaving her fortune to Densher, who will then marry Kate Croy. When Milly dies, it is discovered that she knew of the plot but forgave the plotters, and left Densher a fortune anyway. However, the secret love of Densher and Croy is poisoned by Milly's goodness. Both have changed. Kate's final cry is, "We will never again be as we were!" It is a cry that could be uttered at the end of most fiction.

My novel *Apaches* begins with the following scene. Lieutenant Cutler of the U.S. Cavalry is in charge of a detail of Apache scouts in 1880s New Mexico Apacheria:

Following his Apache trackers up the swale through jumbles of paddle cactus and ocotillo whips, Cutler saw them gathered on the ridge, pointing, laughing, six of them, dirty brown legs under their filthy shirts astride brown ponies, long black hair in turbans. . . .

Tazzi shouted down to him in the Indian way, as though white men were deaf, "Ho, look, white-eye loco!"

Down the swale were two prospectors and their mules, ragged and dusty, with sweat-dark hats pulled low on their faces. One sat on the ground with his pick across his legs and his rifle cradled in his arms, staring down at it as though afraid to look up at the catcalling Apaches on the ridge. The other scrambled up a red-earth cut-bank, not quite gaining the top, keeping his feet with difficulty. He took another run and failed, and he too never looked up at the ridge.

The prospectors are insane with fear because of the torture and death that await them if they are captured by Apaches, in that time and place.

A similar scene is employed at the end. Years have passed, Apacheria has been tamed, the Apaches forced onto reservations, and Cutler is bidding his scouts farewell on a knoll from which railroad tracks are visible. A handcar comes into sight, pumped by two men (as there were formerly two prospectors). They wave friendly hands at Cutler and the scouts, and pass on peaceably. Change has taken place.

This can also be referred to as the rhetorical device *epanalepsis*. This is the repetition of the beginning at the end, repetition in a different sense, or in the opposite order (as above). Any combination can be seen to work at the level of sentence, paragraph, passage, or whole plot.

At the sentence level, from Kafka: "Do not despair, not even over the fact that you do not despair."

Or from Ben Franklin: "We must all hang together, or assuredly we shall all hang separately."

In the Puccini opera *La Bohème*, Mimi's great aria in act one begins, "They call me Mimi. I don't know why." She sings the lines again, on her deathbed, to great effect.

Magnus Mills's novel *Three to See the King* begins with the paragraph: "I live in a house built entirely from tin, with four tin walls, a roof of tin, a chimney and door. Entirely of tin." The final chapter begins *epanaleptically* with the same paragraph, but the situation is entirely changed.

In the film *Mystic River*, the names the boys have scratched into the wet cement at the beginning of the film reappear on the screen at the end, in a changed circumstance.

Strands of tension hold the narrative line taut, the longest strands those of what-will-happen overall, but also shorter strands of what-will-happen in book one and book two, in chapter three and chapter six, as well as in particular scenes. Chapters are hooked together so that the reader is compelled to discover what-will-happen in the next one. If a child is lost in chapter three, which ends with the line, "That night they dragged the lake," the reader is impelled to chapter four to discover what was found in the lake. If chapter four ends with the arrest of the school janitor, the reader will proceed to chapter five.

The long lines of tension are long-term promises, foreshadowings, incompletions implying a later completion, questions calling for later answers, dangers that must proceed to safety or disaster, guns revealed with the implication that they will sometime be put to use, the looming empty space at the table that must finally be filled. The reader is kept compelled.

A note of warning, however: a predominance of long-term promises, combined with a lack of well-developed short lines, will cause the reader to skip, in his impatience to find out how things come out overall.

A predominance of short lines and an insufficiency of long ones may cause too much focus on the immediate scene, with a drop-off of tension when it is complete. This ill is a characteristic fault of short-story writers attempting novels. It may cause the reader to not finish the novel.

A line of tension can be spoken of as a "gun on the wall," from Chekhov's theatrical dictum that a gun revealed hanging on the wall in act one must be discharged in act three. The gun, of course, can be many things other than a firearm. The suspense awaiting the return of the messenger who has been sent off for news will compel the reader's attention. If the messenger returns with news other than what has been anticipated, there is a reversal.

Fiction is a process of change, and the heart of change is discovery or recognition. The long-lost Odysseus is recognized by the scar on his foot, the grandmother identified by the concentration camp number tattooed inside her wrist. Such moments of recognition can become epiphanies. In *The Portrait of a Lady*, Isabel Archer realizes the past relationship of her husband and Mme. Merle upon seeing them together in an informal posture of familiarity. In *The Ambassadors*, Lambert Strether observes Chad and Mme. de Vionnet boating on the river, and understands the degree of intimacy of their relationship.

Tension is created by a promise made, and, after a delay, kept. If a shoe drops from the man disrobing in the room upstairs, there is a moment of suspense awaiting the drop of the second shoe. The first shoe can be thought of as the foreshadowing, the second the fulfillment. The earthquake that will destroy Los Angeles in the last chapter of your novel must be foreshadowed earlier, that gun shown upon the wall before it is discharged. How? Warnings of earthquake season in the papers, publicized cycles, the hysterical behavior of the neighbors' cats, etc. If the catastrophic event occurs without foreshadowing, the plotting will seem inadequate and too obviously serving the author's convenience.

In *The Prince of Tides*, Pat Conroy carefully prepares for a highly improbable scene where a pet tiger kills a gang of rapists. It was a time when gasoline advertising celebrated "a tiger in your tank," and the father of the protagonist's family owns a gas station. He acquires a threadbare tiger to reinforce his advertising, and the tiger becomes a household pet. When the evildoers invade the house to rape the mother and sister, the tiger is discharged like a gun torn from the wall.

A promise, a foreshadowing, and a line of suspense are set up in Nick Jenkins's reaction to his first view of Jean Templer in Anthony Powell's *A Question of Upbringing*. A first shoe has dropped:

> ... a girl of about sixteen or seventeen, evidently Peter's unmarried sister, Jean, was closing the sliding doors. Fair, not strikingly pretty, with long legs and short, untidy hair, she remained without moving, intently watching us, as Peter shut off the engine and we got out of the car. Like her legs, her face was thin and attenuated, the whole appearance giving the effect of a much simplified—and somewhat self-conscious—arrangement of lines and planes, such as might be found in an Old Master's drawing, Flemish or German perhaps, depicting some young and virginal saint; the racquet, held awkwardly at an angle to her body, suggesting at the same time an obscure implement associated with martyrdom. The expression of her face, although sad and a trifle ironical, was not altogether in keeping with the air of belonging to another and better world. I felt suddenly uneasy, and also interested: a desire to be with her, and at the same time, an almost paralyzing disquiet in her presence.

Promised here is a forthcoming involvement of Nick Jenkins with this girl, with her implications of virginity and martyrdom. Or perhaps Jenkins's first sense of her is mistaken, and she will prove to be something else, in a recognition reversal.

Jane Austen's *Emma* begins:

Emma Woodhouse, handsome, clever and rich, with a comfortable home and happy disposition, seemed to unite some of the best blessings of existence; and had lived nearly twenty-one years in the world with very little to distress or vex her—

The reader is assured that in the coming four hundred pages there will be plenty to distress and vex Emma Woodhouse, an unspoken promise to be fulfilled.

Thomas Keneally's novel *Schindler's List* begins:

In Poland's deepest autumn, a tall young man in an expensive overcoat, double-breasted dinner jacket and—in the lapel of the dinner jacket—a large ornamental gold-on-black-enamel Hakenkreuz [swastika] emerged from a fashionable apartment building on Straszewskiego Street, on the edge of the ancient center of Cracow, and saw his chauffeur waiting with fuming breath by the open door of an immense and, even in this blackened world, lustrous Adler limousine.

"Watch the pavement, Herr Schindler," said the chauffeur. "It's as icy as a widow's heart."

In this brief scene in Cracow during the German occupation, we are introduced to a wealthy and influential young man, a member of the Nazi Party, who is making his way across treacherous ice. This foreshadowing and minor suspense symbolizes a greater suspense, for Oskar Schindler, a party member and factory operator, is dedicated to the very dangerous role of saving the lives of the Jews in his employ.

In a mystery novel these contracts between author and reader have to do with the revelation of facts and information, but in the mainstream novel the focus is more on characterization. In *The Ambassadors*, Lambert Strether observes Chad's apartment house in Paris with its fine, continuous balcony, ". . . high, broad, clear . . . admirably built . . . ornament as positive as it was discreet . . . the complexion of the stone, a cold, fair gray, warmed and polished a little by life . . . " The description of Chad's house reflects what Strether will discover about Chad himself, who has been warmed and polished, that is for sure, by Mme. de Vionnet.

In the following passage from early in Henry James's *The Portrait of a Lady*, we have character and plot foreshadowed in this scene:

> . . . a person . . . had just made her appearance in the ample doorway some moments before he [Ralph Touchett, her cousin] perceived her. His attention was called to her by the conduct of his dog, who had suddenly darted forward with a little volley of shrill barks in which the note of welcome, however, was more sensible than that of defiance. The person in question was a young lady, who seemed immediately to interpret the greeting of the small beast. He advanced with great rapidity and stood at her feet, looking up and barking hard; whereupon, without hesitation, she stooped and caught him in her hands, holding him face to face while he continued his quick chatter . . .

Isabel's action in picking up the yapping dog and holding him face-to-face shows us that she is courageous, but perhaps foolhardy and overly trusting of the motives of others. These traits interest Ralph Touchett and the reader in her, and foreshadow her experience as a rich young American in corrupt old Europe.

Here is another example of an author—in this case, Flaubert—doing a lot of things at once, characterizing Emma Bovary, giving a taste in small of the plot at large, and symbolizing her future.

> After the fashion of country folk she asked him [Charles Bovary] to have something to drink. He said no; she insisted, and at last laughingly offered to have a glass of liqueur with him. So she went to fetch a bottle of curaçao from the cupboard, reached down two small glasses, filled one to the brim, poured scarcely anything into the other, and, having clinked glasses, carried hers to her mouth. As it was almost empty she bent back to drink, her head thrown back, her lips pouting, her neck straining. She laughed at getting none of it, while with the tip of her tongue passing between her small teeth, she licked drop by drop the bottom of the glass.

Shown here is Emma's character that will fuel the plot, along with a kind of preview of the plot. The glass of Emma's life is never going to hold much in the way of liqueur or anything else, and she must strain gracelessly to get what little that life holds for her out of it. And she will die of poison with her blackened tongue protruding between her teeth, exactly as it does here.

Ray Bradbury says of character, "give him a compulsion and let him go." Ambition is often the theme in fiction. The ambitious heroes of nineteenth-century novels, such as those of Balzac, have been called "desiring machines." Such a one also is Emma Bovary. So were Don Quixote, Orestes, Antigone, Odysseus, Captain Ahab, and the Joad family headed for California out of the Dust Bowl.

Consider the compulsions in *The Wizard of Oz*: Dorothy wants to return to Kansas, the Tin Woodman longs for a heart, the Scarecrow desires a brain, and the Wicked Witch must have the slippers that Dorothy acquired when her descending house smashed the Witch's colleague, which are Dorothy's ticket home.

See what a compulsion adds to this initial situation: Jack has just graduated from UCLA and has arrived at his parents' house for a celebration before departing for New York, where he will reside with a young couple, Alice and Greg, friends of his father's, while looking for work. His father demands the traditional bout of arm wrestling with his son, at which he regularly proves his superiority. Jack thinks he might win this time, but is defeated as usual.

However, what if Jack realizes that this time he could have won the arm wrestle, but he was unprepared for the consequences of defeating his father? And what if Dad was aware of this? In consequence Dad drinks too much, and brags of his sexual conquests. One of these was Alice, with whom Jack will be residing in New York. Jack has had some conquests of his own, and sees that this is a game at which he can defeat his father, and he departs for New York with a compulsion to seduce Alice. The arm wrestle has foreshadowed a more consequential and compulsive contest to come, with attendant suspense.

Time in fiction is inevitably structural. Time is also an unfailing means of creating suspense. Even such an arbitrary device as heading each chapter with a notation of the date and hour can create a spurious tension. Any stricture on the amount of time available to perform a task, any sense of time running out, can set up suspense. If Bill does not succeed in climbing Mount Washington before nightfall, the skinhead Nazis will burn his wife at the stake. If Maggie "The Cat" in *Cat on a Hot Tin Roof* does not produce an heir before Big Daddy dies of cancer, the no-neck monsters will inherit the plantation.

Note the concentration on time in P. D. James's *Original Sin.*

Chapter One:
For a temporary shorthand-typist to be present at the discovery of a corpse on the first day of a new assignment, if not unique, is sufficiently rare to prevent its being regarded as an occupational hazard. Certainly Mandy Price, *aged nineteen years two months,* and the acknowledged star of Mrs. Crealey's Nonesuch Secretarial Agency, set out on the morning of *Tuesday 14 September...*

Chapter Four:
Ten days after Sonia Clements' suicide and exactly three weeks before the first of the Innocent House murders, Adam Dalgliesh...

And from P. D. James's *A Certain Justice,* page three:

When, on this afternoon of *Wednesday, 11 September,* Venetia Aldridge stood up to cross-examine the prosecution's chief witness in the case of Regina v. Ashe, she had *four weeks, four hours and fifty minutes* left of life.

What of mythic structure?

In Louis B. Jones's *California's Over,* early on the protagonist encounters a coffeehouse called Little Tom's Round Table. Further along he tries unsuccessfully to draw a pen from its stubborn holder. The reader has been warned that Arthurian myth is engaged, and he had better start looking around for some form of the Holy Grail. The Arthurian symbolism is not essential to the plot, but reinforces it.

In Charles Frazier's *Cold Mountain,* the protagonist, Inman, departs a Confederate hospital in the Civil War, heading home. This journey home is certainly an odyssey, the woman waiting for him a kind of Penelope. Inman's adventures do not much resemble those of Ulysses, but the mythic power has been invoked.

Anyone planning a novel of a soldier returning from the war had better keep *The Odyssey* in mind.

—*2004*

"HERE'S LOOKIN' AT YOU, KID":

A Brief History of Point of View

by Alan Cheuse

As we always do of each other, a writer friend of mine with whom I speak more than now and then—one of the most articulate and intelligent people I know—recently asked me what I was working on. When I told him I was thinking about doing something about the origins of point of view in fiction, he responded by saying he sure would like to read about it since it was always an interesting subject to him ever since he audited a course of Wayne Booth's in the early 1970s.

"I never thought about it having 'origins,'" he said to me. "It was just, er . . . was. . . ."

As I recollect, the question of point of view first came to my mind in a writing workshop, the only workshop I ever took, at Rutgers, under the direction of the poet John Ciardi. Craggy-faced Ciardi suggested that we read Percy Lubbock's *The Craft of Fiction*. There Lubbock, an early critical "explainer" of Henry James's work, analyzes and endorses the Master's use of what we now tend to refer to as the third-person subjective point of view in fiction.

That was also around the time when I began to look at movies seriously, perhaps all too seriously.

Growing up on movies makes a kid confused about reality for a number of reasons. With respect to the question of point of view, film gives basically one answer, and it's an odd one. The camera points at the actors against the backdrop of a room or a train station or a mountain range, and they perform. We the viewers are no different than audience members in a theater. But in this case the stage moves just about anywhere, from Montana to the banks of the Ganges or downtown L.A. or the inside of a sports arena or a set decorated as Mars. In this respect we can look at the movies, as a medium, as nothing more than mechanical theater. Eisenstein's genius aside, most directors have the imagination of gifted stage directors, and that's about it. Eisenstein aside because most directors don't pay much attention to the single greatest technical innovation in the history of filmmaking, that being montage. At best, montage is often embedded, or should I say implicit, in the creation of the best movies after Eisenstein, as in, say, the work of Orson Welles.

But whether self-consciously working with montage technique, as Welles seems to have done, or working with it implicitly, as in the films of most of the best and most sophisticated Hollywood directors, the question of point of view scarcely ever comes up. The eye that perceives the action on the screen is always that of the theatergoer, that action having been mediated for the audience's eyes by the positioning of the camera. With the exception, say, of the handheld camera equated with the eye of the main character in a movie such as John Cassavetes' *Shadows*, or, to name another of a very few instances considering the vast number of movies produced in our age, a brief hospital sequence seen from the perspective of the Frederic Henry character (played by Gary Cooper) in *A Farewell to Arms*, the vast majority of movies—let's say about ninety-nine and nine-tenths of them—employ the simple equation of camera lens and eye of the audience member, or the so-called God-like point of view.

The director sets up a shot, a scene, and the camera-man rolls the film, and the image becomes recorded on the film. The editor works his or her montagelike magic, and we get a moving picture. Or the mechanical illusion thereof. What power this allows us to take on as we make the world with our eyes! The lights go down, the screen lights up, and wherever we happen to be becomes as charged with birth as the first day of creation, with the movie audience serving as stand-ins for God.

Unlike the movie audience, readers of prose narrative or narrative poetry find that the God-like point of view comes with a few codicils: Greek epic opens with the poet calling on the Muse to send down the words of the poem. "Sing to me, O Muse," etc. Point of view becomes quite clear. This story about the siege of Troy—this story of a hero's return after the war—comes down to us from the Muse, the Goddess of Memory. If we "see" the story as a god might, that's because we can be assured that this is the way the god saw it. What Achilles sees on the battlefield of Troy, what Odysseus sees in his travels, why that's what we see (as filtered through the image-making words of the god-dess as filtered through the voice box of the poet).

Authority in film derives solely from the technology of the camera and the editing machine. Narrative poetry works in opposite fashion. The poet recites; we take in the words, the rhythms, and conjure up on the "screen" of our imaginations the action of the poem. In the case of the movie machinery we usually get more spectacle than anything else—at best, wonderful travelogues in space and the illusion of time, or marvelously reconfigured fictional narratives or dramas, at worst, a flat rendering of the prosaic imagination.

With respect to point of view, the artist's imagination travels much farther and faster and more effectively than the movie machinery. In the beginning was the goddess or Muse. And then came the Judeo-Christian Jehovah, who, as the implied narrator of Genesis tells us, created heaven and earth.

And the earth was without form, and void; and darkness was upon the face of the deep. And the spirit of God moved upon the face of the waters . . .

The nature of God seems clear from this passage. God serves as the creative force in the universe, about to give form and substance to everything.

What seems unclear is the identity of the narrator. Who is telling us this? An informed observer? A poet who has received all of this news and information and recounts to us now? But if the latter, where did the information come from? From God itself? Or from an interlocutor Muse?

From a narrative perspective something odd has occurred in the shift from the pagan to the Judeo-Christian tradition. The Muse has disappeared, and the narrator-poet of Genesis gives us a recounting but without any apparent means of authority. Where the pagans accepted the Muse on the basis of evidence—the poet acknowledging her and calling on her to give him the words of the poem—the Judaic and later Judeo-Christian audience accepts on faith or the belief in the unseen.

How then does the implied narrator of Genesis derive his authority? How does he know what he knows?

By miracles?

They happen. Embedded in the narrative is the story of the giving of the Ten Commandments, in which God carves out his first-person singular in fire on the tablets. "Thou shalt have no other gods before me."

Of course God talks to Abraham and others. But this is all reported conversation, as powerful as any conversation between gods and men in Homer, yet as secondhand as any overheard conversation in a modern short story. Fundamentalist Christians and certain Jewish sects accept the entire text of the Bible as the Word of the Lord. But aside from the Ten Commandments, the Lord has not put fire to stone and written anything down. To whom has God told his creation story? To whose ears has he pressed his lips?

From a technical point of view the Old Testament is a terribly flawed document that, like the New Testament following it, is something a reader can accept only on faith. But if we look at the Bible in terms of the aesthetic arc of action, we do find coherence—as God's plan for a fallen world becomes clear, struggle ensues, and then Christ the hero enters the action to set things right.

This doesn't happen again in Western literature of any merit. Aesthetics replaces theology. We don't have "faith" in Chaucer or Dante or Cervantes; we understand them in aesthetic and intellectual and emotional terms. After Homer, Greek narrative splinters. But from a technical perspective there is good news. Poets and writers know how to employ point of view, having acquired the technique from the authoritative telling of epic and its variations—mainly first-person, and the numerous third-person accounts contained within the first-person voice. The great classical playwrights—though working in a form that, as Nietzsche instructs us, evolved out of the single masked priest acting out the Dionysian mysteries—have also learned from epic how to create voices within voices (as in the presentation, say, of the bad news about the oracle at Delphi in the Oedipus play, with the oracle's prophecy delivered by the messenger). Just as the masked priest spoke the words of the deities through the mouth of the mask in the mystery rituals, the playwrights deliver their lines through the mouths of the masked actors.

Within a century or two, prose assumes new stature as it delivers the news about the great subjects of new wars and immediate politics. Point of view in the histories is easy to assign, with the writers Herodotus and Thucydides clearly making their own authorship, if not authority, quite evident. But in the other, fictional forms that arise—clearly quite trivial forms compared to history—such as fables and protonovels such as *The Golden Ass*, authority seems both a given and a puzzle. If they have authority, it seems to come from the fact that they once constituted elements of the epic form. Point of view derives from the author, without much of an attempt, as in modern fiction, to separate the creator from the work itself.

This represents a serious break from the early phases of narrative. Without the goddess-Muse to endorse the point of view, the individual speaker takes on authority, as in Herodotus's account of the Greco-Persian War in which, when speaking as a citizen of Greece, he analyzes evidence, assigns blame or praise, and becomes the arbiter of historical truth. Some ethnologists might argue that fables and folktales further the storytelling tradition in Europe as fac-tual or earthly truth becomes the real foundation for future narratives in a thousand-year period.

Unlike modern stories, the focus of the folktale, despite its roots in the earthy and often ribald habits of the peasant population, closes in on a moral. "Wisdom stories" is the way I like to think of them, with their accent on a moral at the end of the tale. But the folktale and the moral tale remain anonymous literary attempts to capture the "wisdom" of the peasant, and thus stand as a form of pastoral. When great writers take over the form, it changes. Chaucer tells his tales supposedly to make some moral point, and he mainly cel-ebrates, which means he shows our species with warts and all, the human behavior that leads to the response of a moral. Boccaccio forgets about "morality" altogether, keeping the form of the moral tale but none of the dreaded moralism. In both instances, the writers present their stories from a general third-person perspective, the legacy of the epic narration gen-erated by the words of the Muse, which, once the theology that supported epic crumbled, evolved into a way of speak-ing about the world that imitates the certainty of deity.

From Cervantes onward, the authority and certainty of the novelist-narrator stand squarely in this tradition. In fact, the way in which Cervantes reasserts that authority by introducing his own voice into the narration serves as one of the pillars on which rests the aesthetic of the modern novel, the paradox of God-like authority yoked to the ultimate inability of the first-person narrator to know everything and the reliance upon the necessity to invent or say what the narrator imagines to be truth. (Here the authority, or flawed version of authority belonging to the novelist's voice, converges with the voice of the poet, as Aristotle describes it in the *Poetics*, telling not what actually happened but what ought to have happened.)

Sometimes that voice may speak in a questioning way; sometimes with reassurance; sometimes, as in some of the eighteenth-century English novels, with a touch of irony; sometimes, as in the modern novel, including the novelist's clearing of his or her throat as part of the narrative voice. That's what appears to be happening in the opening pages of what we all hold up as the model of third-person subjective narration, *Madame Bovary*. Flaubert's statement that he is Madame Bovary ("Madame Bovary, c'est moi"), a declaration we have always taken to mean that he has become one with his character in a mimetic fashion, reads a little differently if you focus on the fact that the novel opens with the first-person narrator describing his early school days with classmate Charles Bovary and then going on to describe—or imagine—Bovary's life to come.

When you look at the design of the story in this light, it appears to be an eccentric, if not badly flawed, opening to a story that is otherwise presented as part of the nature of things. This paradox illuminates both the strengths and the weaknesses of the third-person point of view, a presentation of "reality" that presumes that the presenter, or the novelist, knows as much as the gods used to know. Without the authority of the old gods endorsing the narrative, we are left with the fiction that the novelist "knows" when he or she is really only imagining and inventing. Or, as the great twentieth-century Hungarian literary critic Georg Lukács suggested, the novel is "the epic of a fallen world," in which, ironically, the reader basks in the illusion of the wholeness of the world while he or she is reading, approximating in a literary fashion the sense of natural wholeness that the Homeric audiences held to be true.

What I like to think of as the handbook for the composition of the modern novel, *Ulysses*, builds this ironic awareness of the double nature of the novel's essence—a narrative both "real" and not real—into the essential architecture of the story. The enormous *S* that begins the first word of the first sentence—even before the story itself begins—declares that the novelist is in charge of his own pages, and will do with them what he will, playing with plot and character in much the way that he plays with typography. From that giant letter to the dramatic use of white space in Joan Didion's *Play It As It Lays* lies the path of the modernist novel and gives instruction to writers of essentially realistic fiction as to how they might illuminate certain aspects of their stories and matters of dramatic emotion, as in, say, Jonathan Safran Foer's use of photographs and typographical play in his *Extremely Loud and Incredibly Close*.

The technical matter of point of view becomes, in the hands of the modern fiction writer, as plastic as language itself—a technique to be shaped and formed and deployed as the necessities of the story require. In its modern form we see it emerging in the work of James, as Percy Lubbock emphasized in *The Craft of Fiction*. No accident that the brother of William James would meld technique with the science of the mind and put the stamp of psychological realism on modern fiction.

This leads to a broad tendency among twentieth-century fiction writers to do away with the standard assumption of realism—as developed by playwrights like Ibsen—as a story one observes as if the fourth wall of the scene has been removed, the standard assumption that filmmakers have followed assiduously, if not mindlessly, throughout the twentieth century. Modern fiction writers shift away from this and take up the practice, given the legacy of Flaubert and James, of a sort of over-the-shoulder realism in which the eye of the main character fuses with the eye of the observer, and thus turns around the lens of the filmmaker and points it toward what the main character is seeing at any given moment—the deployment of the so-called third-person subjective. So that what seemed so shocking and jarring in the John Cassavetes movie seems completely natural in modern fiction.

When it's done well.

But of course there are grand exceptions to the convention that third-person subjective works best for making a modern story. In fact, the exceptions show off the modern or possibly modernist vision at its best, as in the way in which the shift in point of view becomes the meaning of the story in Julio Cortázar's "Axolotl" and "Night Face Up" or the vital function of the multiple points of view in Robert Coover's "The Babysitter." Other stories no doubt come to mind, but I'm also thinking about the way in which a shift in point of view has become one of the conventions of the novel, usually from chapter to chapter, with the great World War I tour de force *Company K* by William March leading the pack and Gabriel García Márquez's *The Autumn of the Patriarch*, with its shifts of point of view within sentences, outflanking most other fiction.

Sometimes a great writer will ignore the convention altogether, the way that Tolstoy does when for a line or two he shifts in a drawing room scene in *War and Peace* into the mind of the family dog. Sometimes a fine writer of stories will ignore the convention, as when James Salter shifts points of view a couple of times in a brief story like "Such Fun." Sometimes a good writer will ignore the convention for the sake of an available thrill, as when Ken Kesey in *Sometimes a Great Notion* shifts in the middle of a raccoon hunt into the mind of the lead hunting dog.

Self-conscious awareness of the arbitrariness of point of view has also in the past half-century engendered a variety of spin-offs from classic works, in which the writer chooses a second character's perspective to tell the major story, as in Jean Rhys's retelling of Charlotte Brontë's *Jane Eyre* in *Wide Sargasso Sea*, and John Gardner's *Grendel*, a retelling of *Beowulf* from the monster's point of view, or *Ahab's Wife* and the recent novels *My Jim* (with its story told by Mark Twain's Nigger Jim's wife) and Margaret Atwood's *Penelopiad*, her retelling of *The Odyssey* from Penelope's point of view. All literature is fair game for this neomodernist way of playing. What's next? *Moby-Dick* from the point of view of the whale? *A Farewell to Arms* from Catherine Barkley's point of view? *Their Eyes Were Watching God* from God's viewpoint?

Most new writers slip and slide between third-person subjective and the general, so-called objective point of view, and much of writing instruction is consumed by pointing out where the point of view slips back and forth. A polished, finished story in the third-person mode gives the reader a view of the world from a particular character's perspective. The reader watches the character watching and so becomes godlike in his or her own perception.

But is anyone watching the reader-observer?

If you believe in an all-knowing deity, it's easy to answer that question. If you don't, you have to take a Borgesian leap of the imagination and perhaps consider a clue from the old joke about the woman who, when asked about the force that holds up the world, answers, "Turtles," and, when confronted with a further question about what holds up the turtles, responds, "It's turtles all the way down."

Could it be readers and observers all the way up?

Whose eyes, then, God's to watch with?

—*2005*

A WRITER'S SENSE OF PLACE

by James D. Houston

In our workshops, much of the conversation has focused on personal relationships and matters of kinship—the husband and the wife, the mother and the daughter, the father and the son, or the absent father, or the missing lover, or the seducer, the seducee. There are good and necessary reasons for this. It's the basic stuff of fiction: what we do to each other, and with each other.

I want to focus on another kind of kinship. Each time I drive up into these mountains, climb from sea level to six thousand feet and see this bowl of peaks rising all around us, I get reawakened to the power and the magic of landscape and open country, and to the many ways that certain places can work on us. I think a big part of what makes this workshop such a rewarding experience is the location itself, having the chance to spend a week together thinking about stories in the presence of such majestic terrain. So while we're at this altitude, I want to say a bit more about the role of place in our stories and in our lives.

First of all, I don't mean simply names and points of interest as identified on a map. What has fascinated me for a long time now is the relationship between a locale and the lives lived there, the relationship between terrain and the feelings it can call out of us, the way a certain place can provide you with grounding, location, meaning, can bear upon the dreams you dream, can shape your view of history, sometimes your sense of self.

The idea of place is nothing new, of course. It has been a constant in human life from day one. You can't avoid it. You have to park somewhere, get a roof over your head, and wherever this happens has to be a place of one kind or another. But we're not always aware of it as such. At some point, places move into the conscious life. When that occurs, we begin to have a sense of it, an awareness of it and our relationship to it.

I have lived most of my life on the West Coast, between San Francisco, where I was born, and Monterey Bay, where we've been based for many years. It is clearly my home region, a stretch of coastline and coastal mountain ranges I now think of as my natural habitat. But I didn't always see it this way. For a long time I didn't see it at all. I had to leave home and travel around the country, see a lot of other places, go out to the Hawaiian Islands, go to Mexico and Europe. Looking back, I think I can now isolate my own moment of awakening, when I finally began to see and to contemplate my habitat.

This was a couple of years after we moved to Santa Cruz. I was recently out of graduate school at Stanford and trying to get started as a writer—which involved a lot of pacing and staring out the window.

In an interview once, someone asked the novelist Bruce Jay Friedman why he had chosen this particular career, and he said, "Because it allows me to use the word 'work' to describe my greatest pleasure in life."

"You mean writing," the interviewer said.

"No, I don't mean writing," Friedman said. "I mean brooding, and pacing back and forth and staring out the window."

Brooding, pacing back and forth, I was trying to finish a short story about Sweden I'd started during my Air Force time in England, five years earlier. As I paused to stare out the window, I noticed a candy store that stood on a corner about a block away, on the far side of a large open lot, empty except for a few neglected fruit trees. We'd been living in that house for a couple of years, and I'd been visiting the town of Santa Cruz off and on since high school, so I'd seen this candy store a hundred times, maybe a thousand times. Yet I had not seen it. I'd never looked at it, a fixture in my daily life so familiar it had gone entirely unnoticed.

As I studied the details—the whitewashed walls, the corny Dutch windmill with its tiny window flashing in the sun—something began to buzz, a tingling across my scalp I refer to as the literary buzz, a little signal from the top of my head that there is some mystery here, or some unrevealed linkage that will have to be explored with words.

I sat down at my machine and began to describe the candy store. By the time I finished, fifteen pages later, I'd described the stream of cars along the shoreline road that runs through our neighborhood and I'd described the town, and where I thought it fit into some larger patterns of Northern California and the West. I had begun to examine as well why I had chosen the town and this stretch of coast and the elderly, windblown house we still occupy.

The result was an essay both regional and personal. In terms of my perception of myself as a writer and what I could write about, it was a small but crucial turning point. It was my first attempt to write not only *about* this part of the world, but to write *from* this part of the world. It also turned out to be the first piece I sold to a national magazine, which seemed at the time to validate the impulses that had propelled the writing. It came out in the now-defunct *Holiday*, making it the first piece to earn anything like a significant amount of money, six hundred dollars—a decent fee for an essay back in the mid-1960s, and a bonanza for us in the days when four hundred was our monthly budget.

Since then the sense of region and place has played an ever larger role in what I've chosen to write about, both in nonfiction and in fiction. As far as storytelling goes, I think there are two ways it can work. Sometimes a character in the story has a conscious sense of place. More often it is the writer who grasps the relationship between a life and a locale. In *The Grapes of Wrath*—to take a famous example—John Steinbeck knows the layout of the San Joaquin Valley. He knows the water systems, the fertility of the soil, and the appeal of the soil, and the role of agriculture in the region's history. He also knows the power of the legend that has drawn the Joad family west from Oklahoma. He knows a lot more about this than the Joads themselves know or have time to think about, since they have so recently arrived and their full attention is on survival. A large part of the novel's concern might be described as a dialogue between their struggle and the magnetic power of California, the place they've been drawn to—the natural endowments of the place, the dream that has attached to it, and the irony or dark underside of that dream.

For an example of a place-conscious character I will turn to one of my own novels, *Snow Mountain Passage*, and a woman who is very much aware of where she lives and why. She came to California in the years before the Gold Rush, as one of the younger members of the infamous Donner Party. Her father, James Frazier Reed, had co-organized a wagon train out of Springfield, Illinois. Patty Reed was eight years old when she nearly starved to death in the Sierra Nevada range—right over the ridge at Donner Lake—during the hard winter of 1846–47. But she managed to survive, as did all the members of her family, her father and mother, two brothers, and an older sister. While the others settled in San Jose, Patty Reed ended up in Santa Cruz, which is how I came to be interested in her story. For the last ten years of her long life she lived in the two-story Victorian that is now our home, and in 1923 she passed away in what is now our bedroom.

About half of *Snow Mountain Passage* is narrated by Patty Reed, at age eighty-two, looking back to the time of the transcontinental crossing, coming to terms with her family's legacy and with the riddle of her father's life. At the very end of the novel she is sitting on her front porch contemplating Monterey Bay and a nearby shoreside lagoon. In her hand she holds a childhood keepsake, a pendant made of abalone shell, given to her by a California Indian who traveled awhile with the Donner Party. "Abalone," by the way, is an Indian word first recorded by Spanish soldiers while exploring this same bay, where such shellfish were once plentiful. It's a bit of local lore that sharpens Patty's attachment to the place where she is spending her final years.

I think of mama and papa buried in San Jose, and grandma buried in Kansas beside the emigrant trail, and the generations of my forebears buried here and there across the land, Illinois, Virginia, North Carolina, as well as overseas in Ireland and Scotland and Poland and who knows where else. For a century my people moved, and I have stayed put longer than most. Still a newcomer, of course, compared with those who used to live around the borders of this lagoon taking shellfish from these beaches. Yet seventy-five years is long enough to feel connected to a place. The way a plant will suck up water from the soil to quench its own thirst, we nomad humans suck up something from wherever we decide to stop, and it feeds us. It feeds us. If only we could find a way to inhabit a place without having to possess it. It's possession that divides us, fills the squatter with resentment, sets a man against his neighbor, turns lawyers into millionaires.

Around our shoreside lagoon flocks of waterfowl still congregate, geese and ducks and cormorants, reminding me that a hundred years ago there would have been a tribal gathering place around here somewhere, with so much wild game flying in, and all the clams and mussels and abalone to be collected too. So many lives were lived here before we arrived, and surely their spirits are among us, along the shore, in the mud of the lagoon, hovering above the water, perhaps the very spirit of whoever found this luminous piece of shell I hold. It could have come from our bay out there, where shellfish cling to rocky ledges, gathered up who knows when. It is like an old photograph of some long-gone time, of how the world looked years and years ago, though it is better than a photograph. It moves. It has its life. I move my hand just slightly, and the pearly colors move. The tiny curve of light shifts across the surface like a river finding its way to the sea.

I hasten to point out that a strong sense of connectedness is not typical of the world we inhabit now. The idea that a place can have holding power or be some kind of sustaining factor in a person's life is not widely agreed upon. In fact, it is an idea many Americans nowadays are out of touch with. And there is no mystery about why this should be so. In this country we are extremely mobile. It isn't unusual to move five or six or seven times. We are a restless nation, and we live in a restless era, with unprecedented waves of movement from country to country, from continent to continent. From this mobility and restlessness and uprootedness has come a whole fiction of *dis*placement, which accounts for a great deal of what is being written these days—a vast literary subject unto itself.

Meanwhile, there are still places you can visit in the United States that have been inhabited for centuries by people who have more or less stayed put. At Taos Pueblo, north of Santa Fe, people have been living continuously for over eight hundred years. On the north shore of the Big Island of Hawaii there is a temple site called Mo'okini, laid out fifteen hundred years ago. According to their genealogy chart, one Hawaiian family has provided the guardians for this site, in unbroken lineage, since A.D. 500.

Luckily for the rest of us, histories like these keep alive the idea that a place can have power, sustaining power, shaping power, sometimes sacred power. When voices in touch with these places and their traditions speak to us, more and more of us tend to listen, because there is a yearning now to reconnect with the power that resides in the places of the earth, to remember things we've forgotten. No matter where you live, some feature of the nearby landscape is under siege, the river, the forest, the seashore, something. This in itself forces us to get better informed, pay closer attention, look at what's right around us before it's changed too drastically or perhaps gone forever. The knowledge that we can lose our places has quickened our sense of place. The knowledge that the entire planet is now endangered has quickened our sense of the precariousness of the earth and the need to honor and respect all its systems and its habits.

A while back I was talking with my friend Frank LaPena, who used to head the Native American Studies program at Sacramento State University. He grew up farther north, in a region bounded by the McCloud River, Redding, and Mount Shasta, traditionally the home territory of his people, the Wintu. They have called that region home for over ten thousand years.

Frank is a man so deeply rooted you can almost think the western earth speaks through him. He likes to talk about Shasta, which dominates Wintu country. For him this fourteen-thousand-foot volcanic peak is much more than a dramatic landmark and photographer's delight, much more than a challenge for climbers and skiers. It's a holy place he approaches with reverence. For him the mountain can be a kind of mentor. It can also serve as chapel and sanctuary. He told me about a pilgrimage he'd made to the mountain when a favorite uncle passed away. Frank went on foot and left behind a lock of his own hair as he expressed his grief and prayed for safe passage. For the Wintu, who call themselves "the mountain/river people," Shasta is their final point of contact with this world, their gateway to the next.

When I heard that story I envied Frank and I told him so. I told him that after the Loma Prieta quake, 7.1 on the Richter scale—with its epicenter eight miles from our home—I'd been filled with fear and runaway anxiety and, for a while, a sense of betrayal. I longed then for a place I could go and stand and voice my fear and release my anxiety, make some kind of peace with the powers residing in the earth.

"As you tell me about your pilgrimage to the mountain," I said, "I realize what a yearning I have in my life for that kind of ritual or for that kind of relationship. I wish my culture provided me with more guidance in this area. But it doesn't."

I was astounded by his reply. "You don't have to deprive yourself of that," he said. "It is really up to you. It is always available. You can awaken that aspect of a place, if you make your own connection with it."

"It is really up to you." This was truly a liberating idea, that I could awaken the sacred aspect of a place, or at least open the way to this possibility. What it means is being awakened to a place in myself, that possibility in myself, and allowing the openness to such a dialogue.

The key word here, I think, is *dialogue*. And maybe this is what can bring my rambling digression back to fiction-making and storytelling. Very often "place" functions primarily as setting, as background for the action. That is its role, and that's okay; the emphasis in the piece is located somewhere else. But from time to time you come across a story where the place is profoundly felt, as a feature of the narrative that's working on the characters or through the characters or somehow bears upon their lives. I think of works by Wallace Stegner, Willa Cather, Eudora Welty, Edward Abbey, James Welch, William Kittredge, Maxine Hong Kingston, Leslie Silko, Rudolfo Anaya. . . . Our literature is rich with such works, stories and essays and poems wherein at least part of what's going on is some form of dialogue between a place—whether it be an island or a mountain or a city or a shoreline or a subregion of the continent—and the lives being lived there. It's one more version of an endless dialogue we're all involved in, between the human imagination and the world we find ourselves inhabiting and continually trying to understand.

—*1993, 2006*

COMING TO YOUR SENSES

by Janet Fitch

Some time ago, I had an intriguing conversation with a five-year-old about elephants. "Have you ever seen an elephant?" I asked. "Sure," he replied. "There was a show on TV." "No," I said, "I mean a real elephant. We could go to the zoo." "No, that's okay," he said. "I already saw it." He saw no difference between an actual elephant and a flickering image on a screen.

More and more of us are becoming that boy, typing and tapping, viewing the world through screens and windshields, and never noticing what we might be missing. I remember an old *Star Trek* episode where the masters of a planet are revealed to be naked brains, living in jars of liquid, quarreling and avidly betting on bloodthirsty gladiatorial contests among incarnated beings like Captain Kirk. *Twenty quatloos on the human!* One innately understood these brains' twisted avidity for some kind of stimulus, in the absence of the richness of physical life.

When I think of the lives we're living, here in the twenty-first century, they don't look too very different from those of the brains. We get up to the sound of an electronic alarm, wolf down some unappetizing packaged food, get into the car, and drive to work. We park in an underground lot, take an elevator up to the office, where we work all day in a gray- or beige-toned, soundproofed, carpeted, air-conditioned space, with windows that don't open (if we're lucky enough to warrant a window), staring at a computer screen all day. Maybe we get out for lunch, to drive to another corporate, climate-controlled space, then back to the cubicle. Back to the car, back home, to microwave something for dinner and sit in front of a screen, watching elephants, so to speak.

We were not born to live like this. It's our own affluence and our ability to control our environment that have allowed us to denature ourselves to this degree. We know something is missing. And yet we flatter ourselves to believe that we are the advantaged souls, compared to those who walk in the out-of-doors, who cook over the smoke of a wood fire, who make their own music, who dig in the dirt, who lift and carry, who sweat in the heat of the sun, and who in the cold wrap themselves in quilts and skins. People who grow or kill their own food or shop for it in bazaars full of completely unfiltered sounds and smells and sights. We consider them disadvantaged and ourselves rich. Yet who, in this most fundamental way, is starving? I was twenty years old before I saw the moonrise for myself.

We aren't brains in jars. We crave the richness of the world, its smells and textures and unedited sounds. We are biological organisms who have evolved ways of processing the richness of physical life, and yet, because we have been so successful at controlling our environment, we have eliminated just that life.

So, like the brains in the jars on *Star Trek*, we try to create sensations to replace the vividness of uncontrolled reality. We think that somehow by consuming more and more unappetizing food, more voyeuristic entertainment, more products and purchased thrills, we will fill the absence of that great bath of sense stimulation that comes from ordinary, unfiltered life.

But being human means being biologically designed to be stimulated by the senses, directly, richly, intensely. We know instinctively that the elephant on the screen is not the same as an elephant in the flesh, the way it smells, the hair on its skin, the mind-boggling apprehension of its size, how it makes you feel as its trunk reaches out to you.

As writers, our task is to remind people what it is to be human. Through all the lenses that we embody, we seek to explore and re-create the experience of being alive on this earth. And especially now, in our denatured times, we are in a position to give the reader back the sensual world—restore to him something fundamental which has been taken away from him, something he craves, the smells and textures of physical reality.

And it is not only the reader who suffers from this deprivation. We too suffer the same disconnect. Anyone who sits in a darkened room looking at a computer screen and microwaving dinner shares in the fate of our time.

So first, as writers, we ourselves must reconnect to the life of the senses. To give the reader back the blue of the sky, the heat of the day, the softness of the wind, the smell of newly turned earth, to bring him back to his senses, restoring him to his full humanity, so that he might even think to go outside and look at those stars, smell that earth for himself, we must first get ourselves out of the jar. We ourselves must adopt a more experimental and experiential attitude toward physical existence, and be willing to experience the whole sensual piano, not just certain predictably pleasant chords.

There are five senses—touch, smell, sound, taste, vision—but we live in a sensual environment that has basically been reduced to vision, with a bit of sound added as accompaniment. So, in recapturing the world of the senses, I always like to start with the most neglected, primitive senses, touch and smell.

Touch is the most reviled sense in our Puritan culture, so closely is it linked with Satan and sexuality. *Look but don't touch.* Seeing is alright, but for Christ's sake don't touch—so how could we not be a culture of voyeurs? Watching other people live lives, watching them play sports, watching them make love. Touching means becoming involved. You have to interact, you risk, you take chances. You can't do it on the Internet.

You regain touch by touching. By becoming connoisseurs of touch. When I teach a class in writing from the senses, I ask my students to touch the objects in front of them, usually assorted papers, pens, erasers, purse, tabletop, and so on. And inevitably, I see the most timid fingertip explorations. As if they're waiting for Mom to say, *No, no! Don't touch!*

Don't listen. Take a bit of fabric. Stroke it. Play with it. Try it out on various parts of your body. Try it on your lips, the side of your neck, the soles of your feet, your underarms, your eyelids, and note the variety of sensations. Your whole body is a sensing organism, not just your fingertips.

Take a piece of steel wool, and touch it gingerly with your fingertips. Notice it gives you one sensation—*dry, crunchy, scrunchy, compressible, hairy.* Now, scrub it up and down the inside of your arm. Wow, there's a whole other set of sense impressions—*sharp, painful, harsh, cruel, abrasive.* A leather strap fanned gently against a leg *slides, caresses,* but fanned quickly *bites, slashes.* You discover that touch is not only texture, it's gesture as well.

As you explore, work to expand your vocabulary for describing the senses. Take notes. For example, touch. Some descriptions are literal—*hard, soft, dry, wet, sharp, abrasive.* Then you can move to the psychological—*harsh, cruel, uncompromising.* These latter terms depend upon the attitude of the perceiver, and use the sensation to tell us more about the observer. A girl has moist skin, a literal description. But if we like her, we can describe it as *dewy, slick, glossy.* If we don't, it's *greasy, sweaty, oily.*

Another, very useful kind of sense description is *synesthesia,* using the language of one sense to describe the impressions of another. A great example here is a wine review. In describing taste, one can in fact only directly describe four tastes: sweet, sour, bitter, and salty. But using synesthesia, we can also say the wine is earthy (a smell and texture as well as a complex taste), sharp (touch), grassy (smell and texture, even color), strawlike, and so on. Now, is it literally sharp? Can I cut myself on the Chardonnay? Will I need a tetanus shot? No. But you understand just what I mean when I say the wine is sharp, because you too have a body.

The richest words are the ones that incorporate more than one sense. *Purple* is just a color, but *plum* is a color, a taste, and a smell, even a texture. Notice that Homer didn't just call the sea *dark*, but *wine-dark*. Taste in particular can be wonderfully raided for synesthetic description.

And finally, there's nothing like metaphor. Soft as what? How hard? *The sun beat down like a hammer on the anvil of the hardpan earth.* The only thing that metaphor demands is that it be vivid and that it be fresh. In fact, it must be fresh to be vivid. Language that has been handled too much loses its crispness, its ability to conjure specifics. *Green as grass* will never be as vivid as *green as my Uncle Mort's polyester jacket.*

You can go anywhere with metaphor. And that's what working with the senses allows you to do, go anywhere.

In writing, the senses are prime gateways to memory and the imagination. It's no wonder that all seven volumes of Proust's *In Search of Lost Time* sprout out of the scent/taste of a madeleine dipped in linden flower tea. Scent, in particular, is extremely evocative of time and place—one whiff of canned green beans and I'm back at Wilton Place Elementary School, in the third grade, standing behind Mary Correa in the lunch line and looking at her long black braids, through which her mother wove glossy ribbons, holding my thirty-five cents, always a quarter and a dime. Certain scents, certain fabrics, a bit of music can unlock the great well of experience inside you, memories that are often otherwise inaccessible.

Sense impressions open the imaginative channels. Stories that come from completely unconscious areas of the psyche touched by sense exercises are far more vivid and compelling than stories created from the "neck up": *I'm going to write a story about a girl and a boy in Gary, Indiana, and thus and so is going to happen* . . . Stories that come up through my senses aren't stories that I've invented but somehow discovered, they're already part of me. I take a scrap of yellow leatherette, close my eyes, put it against my cheek, my lips, and ask myself, "What is this?" It could be my mother's couch, or the upholstery of my father's '81 Ford LTD. But it might also be a pair of '70s fake-leather pants, which in turn suggests to me a character, a time and a place, and maybe even a situation. This exercise—taking an object, a scrap of fabric, a scent, a piece of music, a spice from the kitchen, and playing with it, asking yourself, *Who is it, what is it, when is it, where is it?*—is a fabulous way of exploring the inner landscape of your own creative stock.

Take a bite of a tangerine, or a bit of sardine, and try to work your way into the place it came from, to a time and a place and a season. See if you can imagine the shore where the sardine landed, the man who caught that fish, or the woman who sold it. Is it now or a hundred years ago?

I keep notebooks of these sense impressions, always adding new ones, in three-ring binders divided into *TASTE, SMELL, TEXTURE, SOUND*, and so on, dividing them further when necessary; for example, sight requires smaller categories such as *PORTRAITS, LANDSCAPES,* and *LIGHT.* I do this not only because I have a Virgo moon, and like to collect things and arrange them in categories, but primarily, so when I am sitting in an air-conditioned room with a view of the side of my neighbor's house, staring at my computer screen, I can give that scratchy wool plaid to a pissed-off Catholic school girl, or use the sound of the bum pushing a rattly shopping cart full of cans to accompany a conversation on a street corner. It can be difficult to remember, or create out of whole cloth, interesting sense impressions when you need them. That's why "stomachs churning" and "palms sweating" feature so prominently in our fiction. Because the writer is sitting in a room stripped of most sense impressions, except those immediate sensations of his often uncomfortable body.

The notebooks work both ways—they give you a library of sense impressions you can turn to when you're ready to use them, and reflexively, their creation sensitizes you to the richness of the physical world and reminds you to incorporate it into your work. Listen to voices on television and see if you can describe their texture and patterns. Note gestures. Look at art and try to describe the light in paintings, such as in the haystack paintings of Monet.

Of all the exercises one can do for vision, descriptions of light are the most important. Remember that we don't see objects, we see light. When you describe light, your visual world comes alive. Even if nothing else is happening, light is always happening. Make lists of words to describe the things that light can do. Light can do anything water can do—*flow, wash, trickle*. It can do anything an artist can do—*paint, burnish, carve*. Describe how candlelight falls on objects on a table, licks a face. There is always light in a room. You must learn to see it if you are going to recover the sense of sight for your reader.

Once you've worked with the various senses individually, you begin to work them in concert. I find the best inroad is to do the weather. I use my weather notebook more than any other. In your writing, there is always weather. A day is always hot or cold, it's always some season or other. As often as I can remember to do it, I go outside and write the time of day and the date and the quality of the weather. What is happening with the plants? Do I know their names? The idea is to capture the particular quality of this time, this day, this season. What birds are in the air, and in the trees? What's blooming? What do I hear? Nearby? At a distance? What does the sky look like? I have pages of descriptions of clouds. What does the light look like? Are the shadows sharp? What does my street look like at noon in summertime? Who or what is moving about? What does it smell like?

The usefulness of this notebook will become apparent when, shivering through a January storm, you try to re-create July in your story. You might be able to fake it with "hot, sweat, flip-flops, mosquitoes, no breeze," but can you remember whether there were any birds singing at noon? What the shadows looked like? You can't beat "damp underwear, towels stiff from drying quick under a bleaching sun, a wren taking a dustbath in the shade of a pittosporum, the stink of garbage that's been outside for a week, thank God tomorrow's trash day." The more observant you are in creating these notebooks, the easier it will be to stop yourself and ask, "What does November feel like?" The more you look at actual skies and challenge yourself to describe them, rather than settling for generic blue skies or gray, the more likely you will move your reader to look up and see for himself. And he will gratefully turn to your work again and again for that kind of reconnection and inspiration.

In coming to your senses, by re-creating the beauty, the pain, the vividness of living, you invite the reader to fully live. And in trying to be a better writer, you are forced to begin to fully live yourself. So our writing nourishes us as human beings, as we feed our work as writers.

Twenty quatloos on the human! I'll take that bet anytime.

—2006

THE CLINIC

A Liturgy about the Psychological and Spiritual
Distresses of Writing

by Anne Lamott

The clinic has traditionally been a very casual question-and-answer period about the more psychological and spiritual distresses of writing. People who have been in the middle of a novel or story or unable to start something or want to give up or whatever have been able to have the chance to ask questions about absolutely anything at all, questions that maybe you're not comfortable asking anywhere else. Or if you've had terrible experiences with your workshop and you hate everyone ... That's sort of my strong suit. We can talk about that or about what to do if you have a story you love or that other people have loved that didn't get a good response in workshop. We can talk about that. We can also talk about revenge.

I'll just start off by telling you a little bit about my most recent writing, which was the end of a two-year period of writing another collection of essays on spirituality, a lot like *Traveling Mercies*, although this one's called *Plan B: Further Thoughts on Faith*.

I wanted to write another book on spirituality because when I used to have students, which I haven't for a long time, I used to tell them to write what they want to come upon, to write what you respond to when you're reading, when something inside of you, when you're reading something, goes "oooh." That's a really deep signal to yourself that you are in the realm of what matters most to you, and that you can probably write better about that than anything else.

It might surprise you, for instance, that you love certain books so much. I was putting off reading *The Curious Incident of the Dog in the Night-Time* because I was so bitter and jealous about how well it did and it was a first novel. And I just felt like it was a gimmick. It's about this guy with Asperger's, a form of autism. And I finally picked it up. And it's fantastic, because it's about all this stuff that I'm most starved to be reading about, and to be connecting with somebody about. It's about this profound feeling of isolation. It's about feeling very, very overwhelmed and overloaded, and frightened by how loud and bright and unrelenting the world is. And it's funny, and the writing is so beautiful that it gives you hope. It makes you feel like you can breathe again, because the writing is so good, and it's just so honest, it's not gimmicky at all.

But another thing I really love to come upon is spirituality from people who I don't think are total arch right-wing dorks—you know, fundamentalist Shiite Christians. I am so relieved when people will talk about God and spirit and not just annoy me to fucking death, to use the theological term. And I like this size that I had discovered writing for Salon.com, about fifteen hundred words. With *Traveling Mercies*, I'd found that I could use a deadline at Salon for benevolent pressure, which is a very, very important thing for every writer to have, and this held true as I was writing *Plan B*.

Those of you who have actual jobs writing know that there's nothing like a deadline to get the juices flowing. So at Salon I needed to have fifteen hundred words every two weeks, and this will probably give some of you hope and confidence in your own sorry selves, like it gives me confidence in my own sorry self. I am a slow, neurotic perfectionist of a writer. And a good fifteen hundred words, which is about six pages—six, seven, eight pages—can take me one solid week, five writing days. And I start off like I wrote *Bird by Bird*, with just unbelievably terrible first drafts. But usually when I start something, there's something that's been burbling or percolating inside of me. Or I've seen something. I've been paying attention. I think there is either a great story or something that is really important to me. Or I think, God, I love that memory. And then I start to write it, and it comes out really badly. It comes out overwritten. It comes out way too long. Totally show-offy, beating a dead horse, attempts at humor, or appearing to be more spiritual and erudite than I am, as is almost every single thing I've ever written. It's just the way it is, and it's that way for a lot of writers. So if that's how it goes for you, you're right on track.

I wrote only one story in the twenty-four essays of the new book that was not like pulling teeth, and it was a sort of literary photo album of Sam, my son. And I thought this was one opportunity I would have to capture the stuff from the time Sam was about seven until he's almost fifteen. And somebody said, well, why do you want to do that? And I said if I could only write one more piece in my whole life, this is the piece I'd want to write. So I started the story that way. That's the first line of the essay: if I could write only one more piece in my whole life, it would be this, colon, and then it's the story of a walk with Sam in Deer Park, which is in Fairfax, where I live. I wasn't just trying to shoehorn various memories or funny moments into the piece. I really wanted to capture the smashing, crashing, plundering experience of walking with a nearly fifteen-year-old boy, which is to say, I don't mean this in a sexist way, but I'm not sure fourteen- and fifteen-year-old girls pick up branches and smash everything to shit while they walk along. And boys really do. It's very funny: they pick things up and they start to smash and whack, and it's like the other trees are piñatas. And then there's a creek, and this must be addressed also, with rocks. And the piece came out very naturally and organically, and I can say that's very, very rare.

So, a lot of these pieces were things that I hadn't gotten a chance to write about, things that came up during the last couple of years with the Bush presidency, especially since the Iraq war. You keep asking yourself, what do you want to write about? I want to write about how we hold on, how we keep our heads above water, in a time in history when it is absolutely as depressing and scary as it's ever been in your entire life, with no end in sight. And so I wrote about a peace march. Well, how can you write about a peace march without sounding like an aging, Birkenstock-wearing, hippie, middle-aged leftie? Well, why should you bother trying not to sound like who you are? It's really okay. You can only tell us the truth and tell us your stories in your own voice. And it's really tempting to find other people's voices, because if you love something—if you're reading something and you love it—it can be scary how much better the writer seems than how you feel about yourself. But you can only tell the truth in your own voice, and that can be in all sorts of characters: different characters of all sizes and genders and ethnicities.

Anyway, I wrote a piece called "Peace March," and I really love it. And the reason I love it is because I wrote it *so* many times, and I took out all the bad stuff. I took out all the overwritten stuff, I took out all the stuff that's very purple, or too time-specific, you know? I also wrote a piece called "Loving Your President: Day Two," about waking up on a Sunday with a lot of political rage inside of me and then heading off to church. I wrote this for Salon because I want to give people hope. I want to help people keep their spirits, to help people laugh when it's very scary and unfunny, when you feel at your most paranoid, and when you feel that you're just a walking personality disorder, you really feel like you're in an alternative universe.

And so I wrote a piece where I woke up, and I felt, oh, it's Sunday, and I really do believe in God, and in goodness, and in good orderly direction, and I know that Gandhi, and Buddha, and Jesus, and everybody worth their weight believes that you have to love your enemies. And George Bush is my single number-one enemy. He really is. And I have a tiny problem with this forgiveness stuff. I guess I am a reform Christian. It's a group of us who are not good at forgiveness but who still think that learning how to do it is the reason that you were born, and that this is Earth School, where the main curriculum is forgiveness training.

So I wrote a piece about going to church, and feeling a lot of forgiveness, and feeling like I could see George Bush's face at eight years old, and he wasn't this mean little spoiled

Kennebunkport shit. He was actually just a little boy having trouble with his studies. This realm was always a challenge for him. And I remembered someone's face, his name was Johnny and he sat next to this girl in first grade named Lauren, and I'm still really good friends with them both, although I'm much older than they are. Lauren was the smartest girl in the class, and when she was doing her arithmetic, she'd always, for no reason, squinch up her face really tightly, and make this little thinking mouth. And Johnny became convinced that this was the reason she was so good at her studies. So for the whole year, until people figured out what was going on, Johnny Gomez would go, *uuuh*, and make this little thinking face. And you can see that this—and I mean this in a warm and loving way—is what Bush is doing. That when he's signing a paper or when he's trying to answer a question, he's just got this little thinking face on, and his little thinking mouth on. Then he has little special thinking glasses, too, that he wears sometimes. So I started to have this compassionate moment where I thought Bush was actually one of us, or that at least he is actually one-of-us-ish, and if I could write about him with this brief moment of compassionate understanding, that he's one of us too, it would be such a start. Because I *know* that he's going to get into heaven too, and that everybody gets into heaven—but what will surprise him is that you just don't get to choose who you're going to sit at the table with, and I think he will be with a bunch of Sunnis and progressives. But I do believe he will get into heaven too.

So I started writing this piece because in church I got this great title—"Loving Bush: Day One." And I thought, I'll just write about how funny it was to actually feel loving and forgiving and kind of pulling for him to screw up and do a smart thing. So I had a wonderful day. I felt like Mother Teresa, or Wavy Gravy. And then of course I had to leave church, which was where my problem started. But I clung to it for a whole day, and then I woke up in the morning on Day Two, and it was all over. And I just lay there, kind of rocking, and gnashing my teeth, and just feeling the absolute, utter horror of liberals and progressives these last four years. And I felt at that point, having both feelings so strongly, *now* we're getting somewhere. So I wrote a piece that was called "Loving Bush: Day Two." And then I thought, well, in twenty years, are people going to remember how insane life was under Bush? People in Sam's generation? Well, Sam will remember because I've raised him to. But I changed it to "Loving Your President: Day Two." At first it came out so angry and ugly and overwritten, the Day Two did, and the Day One came out so full of shit: so self-righteous and so striving to sound spiritual and evolved. So I took out all of that part, and then there was kind of a funny little quirky human piece in there that I wouldn't have minded coming upon—that says Day Two is not going as well as I had hoped, but better than the day before Day One, which is all we can hope for sometimes.

So I wrote twenty-four pieces that all went poorly at first, like this, and I want you to know this, just to give you hope that I don't start out in the morning any differently than you do. I start out thinking the jig is up. It's all hopeless. The well has run dry—and, plus, all I'm trying to do right now is to get the people in New York to give me a little bit more money before the bombs fall. That is, secretly, what my new pressure is—that I'm trying to get a little more money out of my publisher before the next attack. So I know that isn't a very lofty, spiritual aim, but it's the truth.

So I start out every morning thinking, they're not going to give me any money at all because I've lost and mismanaged whatever literary gift I was given, and this is so beating a dead horse, and I've actually already written these. And then you know what I do? I just wear out that critical voice by getting my work done. I do it anyway. I just do it anyway. I do it because that's what I do. I set aside four hours now, and I can get about two and a half done, two, maybe. I check in with CNN a lot. I do a lot of bribes and threats. I eat a lot of snacks. I give myself really short assignments. I say, if you just write the one part on the walk with Sam where you leave the fire road, and you're starting to walk up the hill now, where you go from fogged-in bad English weather to dappled sunlight to the fierce heat of Greece, I promise myself, if you just write about that transition, when Sam and Lily have dropped behind you, then I'll stop and make you a cup of decaf. So, bribes, threats, the fear that New York will be bombed and I'll never get any money out of anyone, help me pick up the pace a bit. And that's how I get books written.

I'll tell you two more things that I think are important—two more quick things. One is that sometimes you get a really, really good idea for something, or something you very deeply want to do, and it's what gets you started. In *Traveling Mercies* there's a long spiritual introduction called "Lily Pads." It's six or seven major places of spirituality where I landed along the way, from my earliest memories to about the time when I had Sam. And I couldn't repeat that structure or material for the second collection of spiritual pieces, and plus, I'd already said everything that had ever happened to me. But I wanted to write a long, kind—not lyrical—but I wanted to write a long, beautiful piece that was everything that had happened in the last five years. And the political catastrophe of Bush had just about done me in, really left my spirits and soul flattened. My mother got sick with Alzheimer's and died. We lost the dog that we'd had for twelve years. I'd been in a couple of very important relationships that had ended badly. I got older.

And so I got this idea, very lofty, that I wanted to write a triptych, three pieces, including all of the mosaic chips of my life that I thought might hold a tiny bit of truth, or a bit of description that's not overwrought. I wanted to write about the mountains and the ocean and my yard, because my spirituality tends to be based on remembering to go back outside. Seriously, I do not have a single interesting theological insight, and I believe in only three prayers. One is "Help Me"; one is "Thank You"; and one is "Wow"—when you remember to go back outside and go "Wow." But mostly it's kind of this beggy desperation religiosity: "Help me, help me, help me, help me!" Or, "Oh thank you, thank you, thank you, thank you!"

And so I wanted to write this triptych, and I began to write it, and I did it, and it was so—what's the word?—effusive. And shitty. And there was such an obvious attempt to write something *important*, something bigger than its own self. And for that reason it *so* bombed, it *so* didn't work, because first of all, *I* don't even want to read stuff like that. I'll give a book like that twenty pages. So first of all, you know that great Mel Brooks line about listening to your broccoli, and your broccoli will tell you how to eat it, from

The Two Thousand Year Old Man? That is just about the single most important advice I can give you. But my broccoli recoiled, as from hot flame, when I read the finished triptych. However, it actually included beautiful small moments, bits, kind of like if you had a necklace that was very varied, and the beads were all different and from different places, or people had given them to you, or you had gathered them. And if you told the story of each bead, you could probably have something touching and interesting about where you've been and what you've seen. You know, the only story that we have to tell is that we were born humans and we lived for a certain amount of time, and we learned a few things, in the only way that life ever teaches you things—which is messily, and by hitting you over the head, and tugging on your sleeve from time to time.

So I found the beads in this piece, and then I found some whole passages in the piece, and I separated them out, and I took out all the bad stuff. And then there were these stories that were narratives, that began somewhere and ended somewhere else, and showed the person of me growing and surviving, and paying attention, until she got somewhere else, where she never imagined she could get to. Sort of like the old definition of grace, that it picks you up exactly where you are, and carries you somewhere, and you're not the same person when it drops you back off, or it leaves you somewhere where you weren't the same person as when you started. And that's what a story's supposed to do.

There was a mostly reliable narrator in the good parts of the triptych, because I always go back and try and take out all of the lies. There was a narrator who I believed was doing the best she could and who had an interesting lens on the movie camera. And I actually have a good ear for stories, I have a good ear for great lines, and I always carry a pen. I know for a fact that I don't remember a lot of things; I was always spaced out. I was an absentminded six-year-old, and menopause has not brought me the kind of clarity and focus I'd been hoping for. I write everything down.

But if you are like me, you start off wanting to create this golden or tribal community, palace, village, of truth and life that is so intelligent and illuminating, and funny, and quirky, that you wouldn't mind spending two or three years and a few hundred pages with it. But it just does not turn out to be the crystalline glass cathedral or the wonderfully reconstructed Hopi village you had been aiming for. It just turns out to be Tent City in Washington, D.C., when they held peace marches in the rain, and people came, and it seemed like a good idea to bring their dogs. That's what a novel turns out to be.

But if you have a narrator who's saying, wait, I saw this one thing you might find interesting; it was a trip—I actually went looking for one thing and found another—well, that's what most novels are about, right? I went looking for one thing and I found something else. A novelist is asking, do you have a minute? Because I went to help clean up my uncle's apartment after he died, and I found a box of his letters, or legal papers—or whatever—and I found something surprising alluded to . . . and one thing led to another . . . and I discovered something about my family that has changed everything that I thought was true . . . or whatever. This is how stories turn out, not like architecturally perfect structures but like real life, where things can be pretty confusing, but you may see and learn some astonishing things, and there are people to help you.

And with your work, there will also be people to help you to figure out that stuff doesn't work, or that, say, in my own case, may be a tiny bit self-absorbed, or that might be wonderful but way too wordy and came to eight pages when all you needed was three.

Finally, I have this desperation in me, this doglike desperation to show people my stuff, to get some feedback immediately after I have finished a long patch, a bad first draft, and then written another, and then written another. I feel this caffeinated desperation to show it to people, to print it out and to send it to people. And all I can say is, when you feel this way, don't do it. It's a bad idea, especially if you get this feeling late at night. In general, if you have the idea after ten at night, it's a bad one. In this case, you're hurting your own cause. Sleep on it. We used to urge one another to put it through the typewriter one more time, which takes extra discipline and stamina because computers make revisions so easy.

Lastly, if you're a writer, the most important thing that you can find at a writing workshop is not an agent or an editor who likes your story, but a community. I hope you find community. Even if that means only a couple of people whose comments are really smart and cool, who just nail it, who find a way to help you with something that could be really good.

So, two things: find people you can trust to read and edit your work, but hold off on foisting it at them. What you're looking for is not out there. It's something within you that flares up and suddenly understands what you were aiming for in this work, a conviction or a sudden toughness, where you go, okay, I just *got* it, and you push back your sleeves, and you edit yourself more tightly, and go through it one more time. When you no longer feel desperation but you feel like you're close, and you honestly need feedback before you can do a final edit, *then* you send it to someone you trust. The best thing that happens for me is when somebody says, here's what I think, I love it, I think it needs some work, but it's going to be great. And I do this with certain people reciprocally—novelist Mark Childress does this for me, and I can do that for him.

It's very hard to find a place to begin. It's often on about page six, sometimes page seventeen—almost certainly page seventeen, sometimes near the end. Anyhow, what honest, insightful feedback gives me is this confidence that I'm not totally doomed, and a desire, a conviction, that it's in there somewhere, and that I can go through the material again, and shape it properly. It's like when you've let your hair grow out so it's healthy and long, but you need someone to find the shape, and that's my favorite point in the whole writing process, when somebody I respect and trust has said, I like it, maybe there are a couple of things I've marked, and I thought the beginning was actually slow, or it's a little confusing. Don't forget the wonderful Shirley Jackson line that a confused reader is an antagonistic reader. I don't start reading at eleven at night hoping to read some esoteric, high-maintenance Euro-trash existential treatise on something. I just want to find my way into a world that somebody has created painstakingly, where I can get lost, and found. I want to let go and float with the writer, the way you let go in

Event and Meaning in the Scene

by Sandra Scofield

Often, we begin the telling of a personal story by saying, "Something happened." The phrase indicates that we will convey details of a significant event. So, too, must the scene in a story carry the "happening" of a meaningful event. Something changes in the lives of characters, or something important is revealed, or new questions are raised. The scene lays the groundwork for something in the future or makes clear the meaning of something in the past. In any case, the story is moved forward by the scene, which has "zoomed in" on the narrative to spell out the significant action. Its impact resonates emotionally for characters and for the reader.

It may seem elementary to emphasize this about scenes, but in fact, apprentice writers often fill the pages with interior thoughts and muddled actions, or a lot of aimless dialogue, failing to create a sequence of actions that "add up" to something with consequence. (Conversely, sometimes a writer fills the scene with what seem to be big actions, which then turn out not to have really affected the story.)

Event does not have to be huge, but it does have to be important enough to merit the attention of the scene. Less significant events are best skipped or summarized briefly in the narrative.

Keep in mind that "event" is the sum of the scene's actions, which can be spelled out in steps or "beats." This happens, then this happens; it all adds up at a crucial turning point. Characters *do things* and there are shifts in the story. At the end of the scene, we should not feel we are in the same place we were at the beginning. Let's look at a few examples.

In Robert Clark's fine novel *Love Among the Ruins,* two teenagers, Emily and William, fall in love over a summer in the late 1960s. William is intense and reckless, partly because he is facing the draft, and partly because his mother is so radical in her political views. He has come to the conclusion that he has to run away to the wilderness, and he is trying to get his girlfriend to go with him. There is a crucial scene that turns the movement of the novel because William is able to convince Emily that the world is falling apart and that they have only each other. She is scared, but she is vulnerable, rather than self-protective, and at the end of the scene, he has talked her into saying she will go with him. This is a good example of a scene made up of talk in which the talk creates an event: the seduction of Emily. A decision. The meaning is huge: these young people are going to leave their lives for a foolish adventure that will end in tragedy.

In one scene in Ron Hansen's "Wickedness," from his collection *Nebraska,* a farmer is lost on his farm in a fierce blizzard. He crawls into a pen with his pigs and burrows into their "hot wastes" and saves himself from freezing by utilizing their body heat. The actions are his movements in the pen; the event is his self-preservation.

When you look at a scene that you admire—or your own well-written scene—you can state the event. You can list the actions that are the parts that add up to it. And you can describe the emotional impact of the event on the characters. (How do they act and react? What is the outcome for them?) Stating the event and emotion in a scene is a kind of acid test of its clarity and focus.

If you think you are writing a scene, but you cannot identify real action and event, you do not truly have a scene. You might build a narrative commentary on the story, or create a passage of reflection; such writing can provide perspective, insight, and density. But a scene vibrates with movement and meaning, and it is through these elements that you capture your readers. If you want to revise your draft, you have this guide: *actions, event, consequence.*

It may help you to consider what vibrancy or energy in the story is pushing or firing the scene so that it matters to the reader. Unlike tension, which is built from action, this "pulse" is a kind of steady pressure of character desire. Think of the question that is hanging, the knot that is unraveling, the heart thumping. Then make sure the reader feels it beneath the scene.

To make these concepts concrete for yourself, start by closely reading scenes in stories and novels you admire. Choose scenes that stand out in the narrative with an identifiable structure of beginning, middle, and end. Later you can work with more subtle, dense, or complicated scenes.

In each case, identify the *occasion* for the story (why are these characters in this place doing these things?), the *event* of the scene, and the *consequence* of the event, with its *emotional reverberations.*

Also, read widely and learn to identify the need or desire of the point of view character, which is the *pulse* of the scene. Write a sentence to describe it. Look at how it is played out in the actions.

Now apply these analyses to your own writing. Find ways to refine the focus and energy of actions so that they add up to a clear event with a meaningful outcome. Become confident in your ability to engross your readers in the immediacy of the scene's "here and now" moments.

—2006

DETAILS! DETAILS! DETAILS!

by Joanne Meschery

Michelangelo said that great art, "which is not a trifle, consists of trifles."

In fiction these trifles are called details. But then, they aren't really trifles at all. Consider that old complaint about "the devil being in the details," meaning that attention to what some call "minutiae," or the little things, is painfully tedious and time-consuming. But when it comes to writing good and—we should always hope—great fiction, just the opposite of that old complaint is true. It's not the devil but *God* who's in the details. Because details (those little things) breathe life into a story.

Details are never simply embellishments. They serve the narrative in terms of dramatization, characterization, structure, and style. In other words, they are important to almost all elements of fiction.

Over and over again we're told that good, active writing is concrete rather than abstract. It's specific rather than general. And it's in these notions of active writing that details make all the difference. A detail must be both significant and specific. Details offer proof that the story the writer is telling is true (true in the fictional sense). Details convince the reader. They give both the story and its writer authority. This authority, in turn, creates a reader's confidence and trust. One mistaken or clumsy detail can dismantle an entire story for a reader.

The importance of the physical or concrete detail may seem most essential when creating what's called "realistic fiction." It's certainly crucial to writing historical narratives. But the use of strong physical details becomes even more important when writing an exaggerated tale or far-fetched yarn. The reader is convinced to accept the outrageous or unbelievable story because of the authenticating physical details that accompany it.

John Gardner, in *The Art of Fiction*, offers an example of this employment of concrete detail to lend authority to the far-fetched. He quotes from Mark Twain's "Baker's Bluejay Yarn." The story goes like this:

> When I first begun to understand jay language correctly, there was a little incident happened here. Seven years ago, the last man in this region but me moved away. There stands his house—been empty ever since; a log house, with a plank roof—just one big room, and no more; no ceiling—nothing between the rafters and the floor. Well, one Saturday morning I was sitting out here in front of my cabin, with my cat, taking the sun, and looking at the blue hills, and listening to the leaves rustling so lonely in the trees, and thinking of the home away yonder in the states, that I hadn't heard from in thirteen years, when a blue jay lit on that house, with an acorn in his mouth, and says, "Hello, I reckon I've struck something." When he spoke, the acorn dropped

out of his mouth and rolled down the roof, of course, but he didn't care; his mind was all on the thing he had struck. It was a knot-hole in the roof. He cocked his head to one side, shut one eye and put the other one to the hole, like a 'possum looking down a jug; then he glanced up with his bright eyes, gave a wink or two with his wings—which signifies gratification, you understand—and says, "It looks like a hole, it's located like a hole—blamed if I don't believe it *is* a hole!"

Of course, no one accepts that what we're being told here is actually true. What makes the lie delightful and keeps us reading is the pains Mark Twain takes to make the yarn credible. The cabin with the knothole in the roof exists or could truly exist because Twain has made certain to give the place a history and physical features. Details convince us that the man Baker really did sit gazing at the cabin: it was a Saturday morning; his cat was with him; he was looking at and listening to specific things, thinking specific thoughts. The fact that the blue jay holds an acorn in its mouth lends authenticity to the idea that the bird speaks. The acorn falls out of its mouth. Other details help persuade us that blue jays really do think: the cocked head, its one closed eye, the vivid image of the open eye pressed to the knothole "like a 'possum looking down a jug." The reader is regularly presented with proofs—in the form of closely observed details—that what is said to be happening *is* really happening.

Details are definite and concrete when they appeal to our senses. A detail should be seen, heard, smelled, tasted, or touched. And this leads to another function of a successful detail, which is implication. A strong detail can imply many other things that go unspoken in the text. The writer wants her or his reader to both interpolate (fill in the gaps) and extrapolate (complete the hints). For instance, if we're told that a character sitting next to us in a bar has black hair so slicked down with oil that we see comb tracks in it, we might surmise a lot of other details about him. We may envision what the man is wearing, what kind of work he does, the sort of music he likes, how he might speak, or what he talks about. And on and on. This is an example of one detail doing a great deal of work. And that's what the writer must ask from details.

These associations in the reader's mind are fairly endless. Because of this, the details we choose are extremely important. Maybe the writer wants us to make the expected projections about the man with oily comb tracks in his hair. Or maybe the intent is to surprise the reader by having the comb-track character behave entirely against any typical associations that might be made with that detail—in other words, a writer can surprise the reader by creating characters who behave against type.

In *A History of Reading,* Alberto Manguel describes Jorge Luis Borges's reaction while reading a line from *New Arabian Nights* by Robert Louis Stevenson. In this narrative, Stevenson writes of a man "dressed and painted to represent a person connected with the press in reduced circumstances . . ." Borges notes that Stevenson has employed a stylistic device that defines someone or something by means of an image or category that, while appearing concise, forces the reader to create his or her own personal definition.

This kind of reader involvement makes for a more rewarding reading experience. Details gain greater significance.

The reader isn't simply responding to a detail on a strictly sensory level. She or he is now reacting intellectually—possibly comparing, contrasting, cataloging, and drawing conclusions—seeing the significance of the detail and understanding the bigger picture.

In early drafts, the writer may also see details only as concrete or sensory. It's in rereading and rewriting that the more emotional and intellectual functions of a detail can emerge.

When considering the selection and organization of details in a piece of fiction, keep in mind these three criteria: (1) Select details according to the story's focus or theme; (2) Consider to what extent your details (and which ones, if any) will function as symbols; (3) Be aware that important details almost always need to be used more than once.

An obvious example of progressive use of a detail is found in Grace Paley's very short story "The Used-Boy Raisers." The story is written in a sort of fable or fairy tale style. Its opening reads, "There were two husbands disappointed by eggs. I don't like them that way either, I said. Make your own eggs. They sighed in unison."

The narrator of this story sits at the breakfast table with one ex-husband, whom she calls Livid, and her present husband, referred to as Pallid. As the men sit talking and complaining at the table, the narrator, named Faith, is working on a piece of embroidery.

On the story's first page, she tells us, "I reached under the kitchen table for a brown paper bag full of an embroidery which asked God to Bless Our Home." This is the first appearance of the embroidery, described by the narrator with a certain tongue-in-cheek irony. In terms of the story, this detail seems a very obvious symbol. Paley relieves this heavy-handedness of symbol by allowing her character, Faith, to claim and acknowledge the symbolism. She lets Faith give the detail irony. In this way, the symbol becomes the character's—and not the author's—creation. Because it belongs to Faith, the reader is more able to accept the detail's weighty presence.

In the story's next paragraph, Faith goes on to say, "I was completing this motto [meaning 'God Bless Our Home'] for the protection of my sons, who were also Livid's." On page two of the story, as everyone is still sitting around the kitchen table, the reader is given another mention of the embroidery. Faith comments: "Now as we talked of time past and upon us, I pierced the ranch house that nestles in the shade of a cloud and a Norway maple, just under the golden script." Here, the embroidery is gaining greater symbolism and irony, in light of Faith's less than golden situation. Notice the use of the word *pierced*, as if to say the bubble of a happy home, happily ever after, was burst, punctured, the dream broken.

Later in the morning, still seated at the table, the two husbands have moved on to discussing how the children are being raised, then on to subjects of religion, belief in God, and the Jewish diaspora. In the midst of this conversation, Faith lets the reader know: "I had resumed my embroidery. I sighed. My needle was now deep in the clouds, which were pearl gray and late afternoon."

And finally, toward the end of the story, the reader comes to this exchange:

> How do you find the boys? I asked Livid, the progenitor.
> American, American, rowdy, uncontrolled. But you look well, Faith. Plumper, but womanly and well.

Very well, said Pallid, pleased.

But the boys, Faith. Shouldn't they be started on something? Just lining up little plastic cowboys. It's silly, really.

They're so young, apologized Pallid, the used-boy raiser.

You'd both better go to work, I suggested, *knotting the pearl-gray late-afternoon thread* [italics added].

This detail of the embroidery, with its supplication, God Bless Our Home, serves the story in five distinct ways. First, it's an integral part of the story's structure, in that it's repeated four times, serving as a narrative transition throughout. It also changes up the pace of the prose, giving the reader a pause— a more quiet moment—in a story consisting mainly of dialogue. Second, the progression of Faith's work on the embroidery signals the passage of time—the morning is wearing on as these three sit at the kitchen table. Third, this repetition of the embroidery anchors the reader in the narrative. Since the story is one long sustained scene, it's important for the reader to remain aware that the characters are still seated at the table, still situated in that same scene. Fourth, the embroidery, with its request, God Bless Our Home, is of thematic significance to the story. And finally, the detail adds to Faith's characterization. The fact that she's doing needlework, rather than sitting at the table lighting up one cigarette after another, tells the reader something about her. For all Faith's wry wit, bordering on sarcasm, she seems to be a believer, or at least a hoper. She wants a happy home, she loves and cares about her sons. She is patient enough to sit at a breakfast table with two irritated husbands and take up her sewing.

Certainly, repetition and return to detail strengthen Paley's story. But this technique isn't always necessary, particularly when the writer uses an exceptionally strong image. Tobias Wolff provides a good example of how a single image resonates through a story. In "The Liar," the reader is introduced to a family friend, Dr. Murphy, who's trying to help the young narrator overcome his tendency to make things up (or to lie) about himself and his family.

In one scene, Dr. Murphy comes for dinner. The narrator comments: "Before we sat down to dinner Mother said grace; Dr. Murphy bowed his head and closed his eyes and crossed himself at the end, though he had lost his faith in college. When he told me that, during one of our meetings, in just those words, I had a picture of a raincoat hanging by itself outside a dining hall."

This image could be called an "inspired" detail. The leap from an abstract idea of loss of faith to the concrete image of a lone raincoat hanging outside a dining hall is so strong and startling that it can be used only once. But the image is indelible, because it instantly forms a picture in the reader's mind. Just like the narrator, the reader also sees the raincoat. It isn't a cheerful, bright yellow or red slicker. No, it's a gray or dull brown coat. The reader can also picture the hallway where the coat is hanging. It's bleak and empty. The detail is not only physical, but symbolic. It says something about loneliness, about loss of faith, and about the narrator's strong imagination, which he uses to battle his own loneliness, and desire to believe.

One specific and significant detail accomplishes far more than a crowd. The reader grows restless and weary when forced to wade through a dense stretch of details, and the story is robbed of its energy. Katherine Anne Porter, in her wonderful story "Old Mortality," describes the fabled Aunt Amy with only one sentence: "She had been beautiful, much loved, unhappy, and she had died young." This is a fine example of compression in writing. Porter covers enormous territory in that sentence. She tells the reader all she or he needs to know about this tragic aunt. And Porter also gives us the details in exactly the right order. The details become progressively more interesting. She had been (1) beautiful *(intriguing . . .)*, (2) much loved *(could be doubtful, considering her legendary beauty . . .)*, (3) unhappy *(now we're getting somewhere . . .)*, and (4) had died young *(okay!)*.

When delivering details in a list, the writer must hold back, saving the strongest and best for last. A reader feels that momentum of details gathering, it keeps him or her moving through the narrative.

Precise and significant details conjure up whole worlds. They give the writer and the story authority; they convince us to believe. Details help us read, not just between the lines, but they also direct us to read below the story's surface. They reveal characters.

In a conversation between two great storytellers—Stanley Elkin and William H. Gass—Elkin offered what seems a kind of invocation or, in this case, a benediction, not just about details, but the whole of a writer's wondrous and worthy task:

> Let men and women make good sentences. Let them learn to spell the sound of the waterfall and the noise of the bathwater. Let us get down the colors of the baseball gloves—the difference in shade between the

When You Write a Historical Novel

by Max Byrd

Homer started it. Most of us are likely to credit Gore Vidal—
or, if our memories are long enough, Sir Walter Scott—with
establishing the "historical novel" as a popular literary form.
But in truth, made-up stories about real events and people
are just about as old as literature itself.

When my editor suggested a few years ago that I take
a break from writing thrillers and try my hand at a historical novel, I sat down beside a pyramid of books and read as
widely as I could in the genre. And the first thing I concluded
was that Homer's *Iliad* three thousand years ago had established four major conventions of historical fiction that were
still as up-to-date as *Burr* and *Scarlett*.

1. *Historical fiction gives a history of the tribe.* However much it may focus on individuals (Hector, Achilles), the
real story always concerns the fate of nations.

2. *It tells about famous characters that everybody
already knows or recounts famous events from the point of
view of unknown participants* ("His name is Rhett Butler,
and he's from Charleston").

3. *It begins* in medias res, *in the middle of the story,
and makes no attempt to include the whole history of*

events from beginning to end, as a formal historian would. Long as it is, the *Iliad* covers only the climactic last year of the Trojan War, pretty much as Gore Vidal's *Lincoln* covers only Abraham Lincoln's five years as president.

4. *Its scale is long and deep, ranging from the top of Mount Olympus to the gloomy, dismal gates of the underworld.* There is no such thing as a *short* historical novel.

The little that Homer omitted as a convention in the *Iliad*, he took care of in the *Odyssey*, where the first "flashbacks" in Western literature seem to occur: Telemachus sails away from home to learn the whereabouts of his famous father, and the old omniscient bore Nestor tells him in great detail (to the smell of endlessly roasting oxen) exactly what Odysseus did in the war and where he had wandered afterward. Few historical novelists since have been able to do away with the explanatory flashback (or diary or memoir or speech) that fills in the blanks.

What Homer hadn't established permanently as a convention of historical fiction I boiled down to three major questions of craft.

1. *What point of view should you choose?*

This is complicated by a factor that didn't bother Homer: if you are writing about a famous person (Freud, Napoleon, Catherine the Great), do you dare go inside that character's head? Can you really imagine yourself in Abraham Lincoln's consciousness? This was an urgent question for me, because I had agreed to write a novel about Thomas Jefferson, a man whose ideas and writings are known in such detail by millions of people (and who is a personal hero to so many of them) that it would seem arrogant, not to say foolhardy, to write in the first person, from

Jefferson's point of view. Who could presume to speak for Jefferson?

I decided to avoid that implausibility and to write my historical novel in the third person, but then, of course, discovered that I had a further decision to make: Would it be the "third-person omniscient," such as that most Homeric of historical novelists, Tolstoy, uses in *War and Peace*? Or could it be instead "third-person limited," the story of Jefferson's life told from a single point of view, on the model of James Boswell observing Samuel Johnson, or Nick Carraway observing Gatsby? And given its advantages of immediacy and control, couldn't I let my *observer* at least narrate in the first person? Boswell certainly speaks in his own voice, pure first person, in those charming short stories collected in Lillian de la Torre's *The Detections of Dr. Sam Johnson*.

But those were short stories. Most historical novels are written in the third person and from many different points of view—a minimum probably of three, as in Gore Vidal's *Empire*, and as many as a dozen in Thomas Flanagan's epic *The Year of the French*. And this reflects that first important Homeric principle: if a novel tells the story of the tribe and the tribe is to be completely represented, you have to include the obscure and the downtrodden as well as the heroes and princes. You need to have Thersites alongside Achilles, Sally Hemings beside the Master of Monticello.

And a further complication becomes apparent: When you write from several points of view in a historical novel, one of them should speak to readers in a modern voice. Doing so will make a story, though set in a very distant past—ancient Rome, for example, or the Middle Ages—seem less remote, more accessible to modern readers.

Most modern historical novels follow points of view revolving around either a central event or a central character. Michael Shaara's Pulitzer Prize–winning novel *The Killer Angels* simply tells us the story of the Battle of Gettysburg from the points of view (in repeated sequence) of Robert E. Lee, James Longstreet, and half a dozen other generals and soldiers. He uses the simple device of titling each chapter according to the point of view: "Longstreet," "Lee," etc. And most beginning historical novelists would probably do well to imitate his technique.

2. *How do you deal with what distinguished novelist Oakley Hall calls "research rapture"?* Any historical novelist understands what he means: the irresistible pull to learn everything there is to know about your subject, to read every diary, letter, and newspaper, to visit every geographical site, and then to cram it all in, every irrelevant notecard and fact, until your living fiction turns into a ponderous academic history. One solution to the problem is obvious, if like Homer or Margaret Mitchell you have chosen the third-person omniscient. When it's tempting to indulge in grand exposition, to tell the facts without reference to your story, you just do it, as Mitchell did:

> Hope was rolling high in every Southern heart as the summer of 1863 came in. Despite privation and hardships, despite food speculators and kindred scourges, despite death and sickness and suffering, which had now left their mark on nearly every family, the South was again saying, "One more victory and the war is over," saying it with even more happy assurance than in the summer before. The Yankees were proving a hard nut to crack but they were cracking at last.

Or there is a technique I call "cameos and conversation." Ciji Ware's wonderful novel *Island of the Swans* is set in late-eighteenth-century Edinburgh and recounts the story of the life of Jane Maxwell. It is clear that the author has read and seen everything possible about the period and the setting, and also (to the reader's delight) that she sometimes cannot resist bringing on stage, just for a moment, some of that research:

> Framed by the door's graceful moulding stood a well-proportioned young man of about twenty-seven or -eight. The new arrival stared at his hostess with dark eyes that glowed with peculiar intensity as he surveyed the room. His luminous gaze paused momentarily on her lemon-colored bodice trimmed with white lace stitched around the scooped neckline, and lingered a second too long for delicacy. Jane sensed an almost animal-like magnetism about the man she immediately surmised was Robert Burns.

A writer in the grip of research rapture may also indulge in "brand-name brio" (the technique works best for novels set in late-nineteenth- or early-twentieth-century America). You might hand your hero a curious cigar-shaped metal cylinder with a pointed tip (the year is 1895) and have someone murmur, "This is the newest thing in our store, just invented. Doesn't need ink. It's called a ballpoint pen."

To do this sort of thing well, however, the writer will need a journalist's eye for interesting concrete details and an editor's ruthless willingness to throw out most of them. Thus, in researching Thomas Jefferson's life, I found that I had incidentally learned quite a lot about ladies' fashions in eighteenth-century Paris, where Jefferson lived for five years just before the French Revolution. But since nothing is really more tedious and forgettable than dress lengths and wig lengths (actually, wig lengths are good), I ended up using two irrelevant details that I thought would nonetheless please a reader:

a. In grand French homes of the period, the stone floors were cleaned by young men called *frotteurs*, who poured soapy water across a room, strapped two huge scrub brushes to their feet, and glided back and forth like ice-skaters. I open my story on such a scene.

b. For a variety of reasons having to do with the Catholic Church and the facts of life, divorce for a Frenchwoman in this period was obtainable mainly by something called "trial by impotence." If a woman wished to divorce an uncooperative husband, she might make the unnerving, not to say unmanning, accusation that he could no longer perform his conjugal duty, and the husband who challenged the divorce could thereupon be required to demonstrate his prowess before witnesses in public trial. (I'm not going to say how I used this!)

One further dimension of research rapture to consider is a variety of documents as well as voices. Thus, Oakley Hall's *Warlock* punctuates its powerful narrative of the Old West with numerous journals, letters, and newspaper clippings. These can be actual historical documents, copied right out of one's notes (Margaret Mitchell has Scarlett listen to a genuine 1866 poem about worthless Confederate money), or they can be made up by the writer in the style of the time, or they can even be a mixture of both. And because a major goal of the historical novel is to bring a distant world to life dramatically, those authentic voices become a kind of guarantee to the reader that your fictional creation is undeniably real.

And for my final question of craft:

3. *How does the plot of a historical novel differ from other plots?*

My first answer is, of course, it doesn't. Whether you're writing a detective novel, a comic novel, a historical novel, or a warm sensitive contemporary novel about gun-running vampires in suburbia, the elements of plot are always the same: suspense (not surprise), a dominating image that works like a refrain ("Tara"), reversals, obstacles, active characters driven by obsessions.

But it is well to remember that historical plots will normally have one of two relationships to "standard" history. If a writer chooses a story that describes famous events or characters, the plot must be banded and linked by the historical facts. Lincoln dies; Troy falls; unless it is historical *fantasy*, the South loses the Civil War. Yet, paradoxically, the constraint of the well-known and the unalterable can actually strengthen the element of suspense in a plot. The fact that the reader already knows the end of your story somehow intensifies the drama of waiting for that familiar moment to arrive. A reader begins *Lincoln* completely aware of how it *must* conclude, but this only sets the heart beating faster as the carriage begins to roll toward Ford's theater. Or—a double paradox—a historical novel may gain suspense because it cannot change history. Frederick Forsyth's *The Day of the Jackal* describes a hired assassin's attempt to murder Charles DeGaulle—something we *know* did not happen—and yet the suspense is, if anything, greater than if it had.

A novel about famous people or events will probably work best with a subplot about obscure characters, historical or not, whose lives can give your imagination elbow room. A writer, no matter how dramatic his material, needs a little freedom from facts. In writing about Jefferson, I had to stick to the chronological truth about my hero, but I could give my primary observer, Jefferson's real secretary William Short, a private life of his own. Even less is recorded about the slaves Sally and James Hemings—the sister and brother who accompanied Jefferson to Paris, my main setting—so through them and Short, I could strike out into almost any part of Jefferson's world.

On the other hand, a historical novel can exist in very loose relationship to historical facts, if the writer simply sets a story in a historical era and plays out a conventional plot against its canvas. These are the "period pieces" that nineteenth-century readers loved, adventure stories set between the lines of standard history: *Ivanhoe*, *The Three Musketeers*, *Scaramouche*. (The success of John Jakes's *Kent Family Chronicles* suggests that a vast audience still exists.)

Which kind of conventional plot works best? For years I subscribed to the view that there were in fact only thirty-six different plots (from the title of Georges Polti's excellent book *The Thirty-Six Dramatic Situations*). In writing novels for a decade, I boiled the number down to seven, and now, as I compact my natural laziness into ever-denser bundles, I would agree with the idea I have sometimes heard expressed, that there are really just two basic plots in literature. And either one of them works perfectly in a historical novel.

1. A stranger comes to town—which is exactly how *Lincoln* begins, with the new president arriving at the Washington train station in 1861; and how Rhett Butler enters *Gone with the Wind*; and how the Connecticut Yankee finds himself suddenly in Camelot.

2. Somebody goes on a journey—as Odysseus does, and Huck Finn, and Ivanhoe, and even Thomas Jefferson.

But these basic plots always have to be connected to the first and the most important of Homer's conventions: what happens to individuals must reflect, explain, or symbolize the history of the tribe. The *Iliad* tells Greeks why Troy is no more. *Lincoln* tells Americans why the nation was reborn, in bloody union. I chose to write about Thomas Jefferson because, in his words and imagination, he could almost be said to have invented America and the idea of a democratic republic. Lesser lives, like that of Huck Finn, also have to be woven into the big world—in Huck's case, the world of antebellum slavery—and not permitted to exist unconnected to the life around them. That is why increasingly I have come to think of historical fiction as a healthy form for the inward-looking, self-absorbed modern imagination to take.

—1993

MAKING WORKSHOPS WORK

by Sands Hall

The workshop begins. Perhaps you've met an instructor and some of your workshop peers and have an idea of what the expectations are for the weekend, the week, the next semester. Perhaps you've also been handed a number of manuscripts.

Now what do you do? What does the workshop—not to mention the author whose work is under examination—expect from you?

The pros and cons of the workshop system have been and will continue to be debated, but it remains an honored method of improving a writer's craft, both through feedback received on a piece of writing and as a way to hone a writer's skills. It is perhaps the second half of this equation that is the most surprising, and the most valuable.

A workshop consists of a group of people, each of whom brings some literary understanding to the table, gathered to tell each other what is working and what is not in some pages of their writing, and in the process to explore, uncover, and discuss aspects of writers' craft.

We must do this with a great deal of respect: for the work and for the endeavor. After your writing—consisting of an entire story, pages of a longer manuscript, or an assigned exercise—has been critiqued, you will want to return to your yellow pad, your typewriter, your computer screen, with enthusiasm. And this is true of your fellows: they too will want to return home excited to continue; and that encouragement is part of the task of the workshop. This will be accomplished through respect, and the earnest desire to help each writer and his or her manuscript improve.

In addition to the pragmatic opportunity to receive feedback on a piece of writing, writers seek out workshops for other reasons: for inspiration, or to experience a sense of community, rare in our vocation. Or we seek assistance: We may begin a piece with the entire arc of a story clear in our minds, but as we continue to write, this clarity vanishes. Sometimes we have a terrific beginning, but then what? Sometimes we have an ending in mind and try to force our characters into actions to fulfill this final image. However it happens, all too often, in the process of stringing sentences together, we grow frustrated—and our story, short or long, slips from our grasp. In this regard workshops can be very helpful. They can help us recover the original germ of a story that has gotten lost; can assist with an ending that doesn't pull together; and, perhaps most valuable, can help us find the story we didn't know we were telling.

Above all, through the process of critiquing manuscript after manuscript, a workshop gives a writer insight into art, craft, and technique that she takes home to her own continuing work.

Remember that the manuscript is why you are in a workshop. This vital detail often gets lost, especially in a short week that may offer lectures and panels, meetings and connections. Those sheets of paper—over which you and your fellow writers have slaved—often get put to one side; they can even become a secondary activity. If you are part of an ongoing writers' group, or in a class, which meets every one or two weeks, life itself can intervene. But in fact, you are in a workshop because of the manuscript. You are there to have yours discussed; you are there to read, critically, the manuscripts of others.

Criticism: To criticize

Too often, we apply this word in a limited sense: to react to something negatively. This is particularly true in a workshop, where a red pen, so to speak, is already in hand even before the reading begins, with the purpose to "find what isn't working," rather than what is. Courtesy of Webster's, let's look at other meanings of these words:

CRITICAL: Marked by careful and exact judgment and evaluation.

CRITICISM: The art, skill, or profession of making discriminating judgments, especially of literary or artistic works.
Note: This does not say *negative* judgments, but, rather, *careful* and *discriminating* ones.

DISCRIMINATING: Capable of recognizing or making fine distinctions: perceptive.

Thus, a workshop gives a group of perceptive people the opportunity to make perceptive comments and discriminating judgments of literary work. It is not a place to practice shredding, scalping, and ego-blasting. Nor is it a contest in being "nice." And if someone said nasty things about your manuscript yesterday, swallow your pride and your urge for revenge and attend to your work today, even if it means pointing out excellence in that person's work.

Here is this amazing thing: the more thoroughly you read the manuscripts of others, the better your own editorial eye will become, and this, above all, is what you take back to your own work. I have read that the Sanskrit root of the verb *to judge* means *to separate the wheat from the chaff.* This might be a valuable resonance to keep in mind when your head is reeling at the end of a workshop.

And now to some pragmatics.

Preparing a manuscript for discussion in a workshop

When you first sit down with a story or a section of a novel, read it at least twice, the first time without a pencil or pen (of whatever color) in your hand or criticism in mind. Read it all the way through at one go—don't break up your concentration or your criticism will be similarly fragmented. Give it the kind of attention you would a story in a literary magazine or a book a respected friend has lent you. For example, try not to leap to immediate and negative judgments about authorial idiosyncrasies; these just might turn out to represent a personal and distinctive writing style.

Then take a few moments to think about the effect the story or novel segment created. Give yourself time to do this job well. *This is what each of you has joined the workshop to receive: a detailed, thoughtful analysis of your manuscript.*

Things to think about

Characters:

Do you care about them? Well-drawn characters aren't necessarily likable, but has the author succeeded in having you engage with them?

Are they fleshed out adequately?

Does the author succeed in making them unique?

Or are they walking clichés?

Do their motivations make sense and drive them through the story?

Are they consistent in their actions and their dialogue? If not, do these inconsistencies tell you something about them, or about the plot?

Plot:

What happens?

Does someone change?

Is the story or chapter intriguing; did the writer succeed in creating a sense of tension?

It might be helpful to keep in mind that plot is not only what happens, but also the order in which a reader *discovers* what happens. Sometimes a simple summary of the plot can be helpful to the writer and may lead to other questions: Does the story or chapter start before it needs to? Are scenes included that are not necessary? (See "Language" and "Detail.")

Point of view

Is the piece written in first person? Third person? Changing or rotating? Omniscient?

Is the point of view consistent? Are there changes in perspective that are jarring?

Does the point of view chosen to tell the story seem to be the most effective one possible?

Are vocabulary, grammar, even punctuation consistent with the nature of the chosen point of view?

Voice

(see "Point of view" and "Language")

Is the voice consistent, or does it waver?

Did you find it intrusive, or was it right for the story being told?

Language

Is the author's language elegant? Realistic? Vivid, boring, cerebral? (Clearly, this contributes to the quality of the voice.)

Is the language true to the narrator, the point of view telling the story? Or is it the language of the author? (This may be a matter of "style," not necessarily more or less effective, but it's good to note: either way, is it purposeful?)

Is the writer's use of language clichéd, or do interesting turns of phrase strike you with their unique take on the world?

Does the author use strong verbs?

Are figures of speech used unusually and well?

Here is Ezra Pound's advice to Ernest Hemingway:

Use no superfluous words.

No adjective that does not reveal something.

Go in fear of abstractions.

Detail

Does the author use detail well?

Are the details intrinsic to the characters and story, or does their inclusion seem merely "writerly"?

Does a given detail advance character? And/or plot? And/or theme?

You might examine the writer's use of *metaphor*: do objects and incidents in the manuscript represent more than their "surface" meaning? Are these consistent with the thematic concerns of the story?

Dialogue

Is it believable?

Is it appropriate to the characters and to the style of the story?

Does it help to round out the characters?

Is there too little dialogue?

Is there too much: does the author depend on characters to literally tell the story?

Is any dialogue-as-exposition handled deftly? Awkwardly?

Is there a dependence on adverbs in the attributions (*he said, calmly; she commented, angrily*; or—my favorite—*she asked, interrogatively*) to communicate tone? That is, does the author TELL or SHOW how the characters are behaving?

Content

Is this a story you've read before?

Or does it give you a fresh look at the world, asking you to think about something in a new way?

Would you like to read more about this world, or by this author?

If the manuscript is a chapter in a novel, would you want to read on?

Theme

What is the story—or the chapter—about?

Does the writer seem to begin with one idea and then veer into something unconnected?

Do the elements listed above contribute to your understanding of the theme, or does the writer's choice of details, style, characters, etc., confuse you?

(Some authors maintain that they are not interested in theme, or that if there is one, it is not "purposeful"; this is disingenuous. Any worthwhile discussion of a manuscript includes the ideas it provokes, and it behooves the writer to sooner or later become aware of what those are.)

Title

Does the title of the story or novel contribute to your understanding of the pages you've read?

Does it offer a "key" as to theme, or how the author might intend you to read the manuscript?

After you've pondered these elements, then heft your pencil or pen and get to work. Reread the manuscript, marking places and phrases that worked for you as well as ones that didn't, and—this is a great help to the author—write commentary in the margins as to *why*. This is an opportunity for you to communicate directly with the author, and perhaps as important, a great exercise in figuring out why you like or dislike certain kinds of writing.

Some readers like to create a key: a check mark or some squiggle lines for something that is particularly effective; a question mark beside something that doesn't make sense; parentheses around a phrase or section that seems redundant and can be deleted. I had a reader who would write, simply, "Fix," in the margin of a bad section, or, less helpfully but cogently, "Snore."

I ask the students in my own workshops to write a paragraph or two giving their overall response, and some participants come to class with a page of typewritten notes, work that is very much appreciated by the author under discussion. However you go about this preparation, determine a thesis of sorts: what you did and did not like about the story, and about the writing. Substantiate your points with specific examples—specificity and detail are as vital in criticism as they are in writing. In other words, *generate an opinion before you come to class.* This will keep you from being swayed by what seems to be the "overall consensus" of the workshop, all too often the view of one or two articulate and opinionated participants.

These prepared critiques will also force you to examine what you think good writing is, as well as why you think so, which is one way we begin to figure out what our own writing style is. Above all: *The more thoroughly you apply yourself to the task of intelligent criticism, the more your perception of writing will expand.*

In writing workshops, the Golden Rule applies, and it is helpful to address what you think the writer is doing *well*— what it is about the manuscript that you think "works"— and, when it's time to discuss the manuscript's less successful attributes, to be respectful. Don't rewrite the story. Don't discuss stories or novels that it's "like." Your criticism and suggestions should address what already exists, with the goal of making it as good as possible. It helps to keep this idea in mind: What was the writer going for? How well did she accomplish what she set out to do?

Some of the participants in your workshop may be working in a particular genre—historical fiction, romance, "chick lit," speculative fiction (sci-fi), fantasy. Avoid any tendency to precede your critique with "I never read this sort of thing" or "This isn't my cup of tea," comments that immediately create defensiveness in the author as well as in those whose cup of tea such fiction happens to be. Our job is to take what's on the page and make it effective—that is what everyone is there to accomplish. Remember, literary fiction is a genre too.

The person whose manuscript is being critiqued is depending on your attention and looks forward to the insights that you, specifically, have to offer. For this reason, flip, sarcastic comments are not welcome, neither in class nor on the page. It is all too easy to be arch and wryly brilliant while demolishing someone else's writing. I'd like to believe this sort of teaching/workshopping is old-fashioned in any case; it reminds me of the ballet master in one of Degas's paintings, who holds a long stick with which to rap the unaesthetic calves and awkward arms of an erring ballerina. There are other ways to assist a person toward effective art.

Be sure you sign your name to your critiqued manuscript. At the end of his or her workshop the writer gets these critiques back, and it is helpful to relate written criticisms to what got mentioned (or, as often happens, what did not) during class discussion.

If for some reason you are not called upon in a workshop to voice your opinion, it is up to you to raise your hand and do so, especially if the class consensus is moving in a direction that diverges from your own. All too often, the writer being workshopped gets her critiqued manuscripts home and, upon reading through them, discovers that what seemed to be the opinion of many was actually the (loud) determination of a few. Speaking up is part of being a "good" (meaning productive and contributing) workshop member. It is a responsibility. If you feel something is being praised too highly or criticized too much, dare to say so! Sometimes the discussions that erupt from these disagreements can be explosive, but they are almost always illuminating.

It is also possible that in the course of a good discussion you might have your mind changed.

For the purposes of discussion, *it is extremely useful to talk about the writer and the work being critiqued in the third person.*

This takes a bit of getting used to, but it is a worthy discipline. The author does not have to feel, as author/teacher James Frey puts it, as if he is in the docket answering charges. Rather than worrying if he's acknowledging the person who's speaking, or demonstrating that he's taking it well, the author can concentrate on listening to the criticism. This keeps criticism from being given—or taken—personally, and encourages a discussion of *literature*, rather than a personal take on the work under examination.

Never assume that something written in the first person, or even third, is autobiographical. Never address the writer as if he is the narrator (as in "I was troubled by that section in which you slept with that awful woman").

For the writer whose work is being discussed

Above all: *Listen to what is being said. Do not enter into the discussion of your manuscript.* Even nodding or wincing or shaking your head may alter important perspectives that might not, as a result of your reaction, be articulated.

Bring a notebook and jot down the points that come up during your workshop. This serves several purposes. It helps you remember excellent ideas that might otherwise slip away in the heat of the moment. It can also keep you from getting defensive. (You can scribble your snide comments into the notebook.) In addition, when the time comes to rethink and then rewrite, you can refer to these notes.

It's very important that *you do not defend your story*, even to yourself, much less out loud. If something isn't clear to your readers, no matter how obvious you may think it is, then rest assured it is not in your manuscript. In any case: Your goal in a workshop is not to explain your story, but to witness what readers are getting out of what you wrote. When the book is open in a reader's hands in a living room, a plane, a bedroom, you will not be there to explain what they do not "get."

After a workshop is over, you might want to take a clean or relatively unmarked copy of the manuscript and cull the comments your readers have made onto this one copy. When the time comes to rework the piece, you have all the criticism in one place. This also gives you an opportunity to examine all the responses together and see where there is a consensus of opinion. However, sometimes one reader may mark a passage "YES!!! *LOVE* THIS!!" and another might draw lines through the same section and write "DELETE—BUMS ME RIGHT OUT." In this case—and it happens often enough—there is clearly something exciting going on. It is up to you to decide what's caused the variety of reactions. While it may be the result of something confusing, it may also be at the heart of your story, something from which the story may actually benefit.

Whenever possible, give yourself a good amount of time away from a story or chapter section before beginning a rewrite of your critiqued pages. The space and time allow the dust to settle. You will remember and synthesize the salient criticisms and forget those not vital to your rewrite.

And remember, it is your story. Keep in mind what you are going for and stay true to that endeavor. Sometimes it's a tough balance, but it's worth fighting for; listen well, but keep your own counsel.

Regarding novel segments

Unlike a short story, which is a self-contained unit, a novel segment cannot and should not answer all of a reader's questions. In fact, a novel must consistently accomplish the opposite of this: generate enough mystery that the reader continues to turn the pages.

We need to keep this in mind when we critique a section of a novel. The lack of resolution in these pages may very well be part of a longer arc the author is purposefully creating. Often the questions we wonder about—Why does Margie get mad at Jim when he mentions babies? Why does Phoebe keep thinking about her sister? Why does the author include sections in which a tortoise makes its way across a road?—are exactly the ones the author wants us to ask. Creating the desire to know what happens next is the essential task of the novelist.

However, this is not the same as confusing the reader. If you find yourself wondering whether or not the writer has thought of certain issues, mention them! Certain ramifications of plot, character, image, metaphor, etc., may not be clear to a writer until they have been pointed out. Sometimes these revelations are exciting and feed the direction in which the book is already going. Sometimes they create a need to rethink and rewrite. The author may be appalled at what certain readers think items or activities signify. On the other hand, she may be deeply gratified that her readers are "getting" what she has so carefully layered into her manuscript. Readers' insights of this kind are very valuable.

If a novelist is making you want to know more, acknowledge that he is doing so. Similarly, let him know, respectfully, if he is not succeeding at this essential task.

For the person receiving criticism on a novel segment

Again and again you will be tempted to say "Oh, that's in the next section" or "I covered that in chapter three." If the questions brought up in a workshop do happen to be answered elsewhere, nod sagely and pat yourself on the back: you've done your work. If the questions raised are ones that startle you, or the ramifications are different than what you intended, try not to get defensive. In either case, *listen. Take notes.* Ideas will be presented that you haven't considered and that you might be inspired to include.

Sometimes readers point out problems: "This moves slowly; there's too much unneeded detail." "The character seems strident." "The writing is choppy." It's probable these criticisms are pertinent to the novel or to your writing as a whole. Try to take the specific criticism and apply it to your work in a general way.

Regarding workshop leaders, and the occasional "bad" workshop

Difficult though it may be, particularly if your workshop leader is famous, and/or articulate and/or opinionated, remember that his or her opinion is only one opinion, albeit an experienced one.

Workshop leaders are expected to have done their own preparation and have usually developed their own style and methods. It is not uncommon to set up the class so that the discussion moves around the room, with each participant in the workshop given the opportunity to offer an opinion. Once the members of the workshop have warmed up to each other and to the work at hand, the discussion often takes on its own momentum. It may be easier, if you are shy, to sit back and let the voluble do the talking, but that is not what you are in the workshop to do. You are there to probe and discuss and, above all, to realize your own opinions about what makes a piece of writing work. This takes active participation.

Every workshop leader has something very particular to say about the process of writing. Something can be gleaned from every workshop and every teacher. Sometimes a workshop that seems harsh at the time will result in a series of valuable improvements in your writing.

You may get a workshop leader with whom you have an immediate affinity; you may have one who seems downright mean, and, of course, anything in between. Sometimes lessons are hard-learned. I think it's possible to get them without being devastated. But if your workshop is tough— and sometimes, no matter how good the intentions of all involved, it can be—take heart. There is probably a good lesson in there, and if you keep writing you will usually figure out what it is.

Which leads me to say: Sometimes we come to a workshop and offer up our manuscript as if it is our very heart. Sometimes our life seems bound up in the three to five thousand words we present to our peers. But do not expect that everyone, or even anyone, will see in your pages all the care that you have lavished there. We can feel destroyed by the casual—no matter how respectful—attention our pages may receive. Be prepared for this. Your life will probably not change as a direct result of your workshop. But, if you pay attention to the critique of your own manuscript, and are careful and thorough with your critiques on the manuscripts of others, your writing will change, and then, perhaps, your life will too.

Writers' workshops, writers' conferences, can be very intense times. Souls are often exposed—in stories and around those manuscript-littered tables. Sleep well. Eat well. Take care of yourself, and of your peers.

In conclusion

A workshop may be ongoing: a group of writers who live in close proximity and meet every few weeks; a course that extends over days, a week, a semester. While working with your peers you have the opportunity to come to know those whose opinions and insights you particularly respect, and who seem to understand what you are trying to do with your writing. Perhaps this one, or these few, may be willing to continue to work with you. If you don't live in the same area, you can exchange manuscripts by mail, or e-mail critical perspectives to each other, and make arrangements to read manuscripts and then talk on the phone. Some find a way to meet in an agreed-upon place for a few days every year to write and work together. Many legendary literary friendships have sprung up out of this mutual regard. If you are lucky enough to find those who will work with you in this way, you join an honorable tradition.

An effective workshop is usually the result of collaborative hard work. It is also tremendously exciting and often fun. It requires discipline, especially in a weeklong conference, when in addition to lectures, readings, ancillary outings, and spontaneous talks with staff and fellow participants, you must critique at least two manuscripts a day. But those who thoroughly apply themselves to the task of intelligent, careful criticism begin to appreciate how writers *work*. They uncover techniques, ideas, connections that invariably illuminate their own writing.

This has been a revelation to any number of workshop participants. They tell me that while it was interesting and helpful to receive responses to their own manuscript, what they actually garnered from the workshop process was *the development of their own critical faculties*. These gleanings of art and of craft, and above all *the ability to criticize a manuscript effectively*, will be applied, in the future, to their own work.

—2006

REFLECTIONS ON SCENE AND SUMMARY

by Al Young

If you wanted the sky I would write across the sky in letters,
That would soar a thousand feet high,
"To Sir, With Love."

—"To Sir, With Love," words by Don Black, music by
Marc London (as sung by Lulu)

It wasn't until I got hired to write scripts in Hollywood that
I began to pay close attention to the ways a checkered balance of scene and summary moves a story along. Narrative—fictional or so-called nonfiction—leans on dramatic
enactment and the strategic contraction of time; each plays
off the other.

Good screenwriters, memoirists, poet-narrators, novelists, or real-time raconteurs all know how and when to para-
chute out of the cloud-blown sky of summary back to solid
ground. It is the specific, particular grounding moments that
advance a story line, or deepen or clarify a story's meanings. To onlookers and eavesdroppers, a scene suggests that

whatever we see and hear unfolding, whatever is happening, *must* unfold in this unalterable way. A scene is dramatically layered and pocked with detail, idiosyncratically nuanced, and redolent of the worlds through which characters move, to say nothing of the situations or predicaments on which the story turns. The sensual imagination always craves an event to witness, to take in, to see. Scene. Seen. Touched. Heard. Held. Hit. Chased. Shot. Rescued. Kissed.

I began following the trail toward this end one morning when I turned up at actor-director Sidney Poitier's house in Beverly Hills to begin our workday. He had hired me to write a script based on an idea he had for an action comedy. Sidney liked to talk-tell his stories. My job was to listen and take notes. He even let me tape these sessions, although he later asked me to turn the recordings over to him. We usually worked from nine to three, breaking for lunch, then I would go back to the Sunset Hyatt, which I'd chosen because a lot of touring musicians stayed there.

In the lobby or restaurant-bar I could watch some joker yawn and stretch and tell his group: "Hey, I'd love to hang with y'all for the rest of the night. But (*yawn, yawn*), I got to be over at the Bowl early tomorrow to start setting up for Donna Summer and the O'Jays." Or you could walk up Sunset to the Rainbow Grill and, in mid-meal, catch Linda Ronstadt dash in, clad in what looked like a nightgown and a robe, to pick up a to-go order. Patrons would pretend to ignore her. But the moment she left, somebody would holler: "Did you see that? That was Linda Ronstadt." It was Hollywood and, to paraphrase the legendary Jimmy Durante, everybody made sure they got into the act. The point, of course, in telling you all this is to toy with a bit of scene and summary in action.

Up in my room, I would study my notes and listen to Sidney on tape. Sometimes, when he made up characters, he gave them speaking voices, and even lines of dialogue. But only sometimes. After all, I was the scriptwriter. I would crank out pages for Sidney to take with him the next day into a room off of the study with a closable door. Who wants to be watched while he's reading? Still, I could hear Sidney. More than once I would hear him break up with laughter, yet he would come back into the study coolly composed. "Funny stuff," he would say, treating me to his seriously engaging *Lilies of the Field* look. "But it could be funnier—and crisper."

There came a morning when Sidney stepped back into the study, clutching my pages, and looked down at me dolefully.

"Al," he said, "you hogged up a lot of pages with exposition. You took up way too much space, telling what happened here and what happened there. Why don't you just do it in a scene? I'm not a writer, but I can tell you when something in a script isn't working."

Weeks slithered by before I turned in the completed script, and then it was I who was no longer working. That untitled story-in-process eventually became the hit film *A Piece of the Action*. By my hand-to-mouth freelancer measure, I was paid handsomely for my contribution, but it was my successor, Richard Wesley, originally a stage playwright, who snared the solo screen credit. What I learned from that experience I applied to subsequent scripts I was invited to write, and my fiction began to take bold turns.

That film technique owes much to literary storytelling is hardly a secret. Early film versions of theatrical stage plays were shot the way a high school or college audiovisual squad shoots DVDs or videos of visiting speakers. The camera was set up in one fixed spot—the place chosen by the director. I find this analogous to the old-fashioned authorial style of storytelling, where the writer of the story hovers over depictions, characterizations, and unfolding events so fixedly that readers must swim or sink.

In 1885, after he and his brother Auguste invented the cinematograph—a portable version of the massive movie camera Thomas Edison would come up with three years later in New Jersey (Edison called his invention the kinetograph)—Louis Lumière declared: "The cinema is an invention without a future." After all, he reasoned, why would people pay to see stuff they could see in real time, out on the streets or all around them, for free?

As techniques of film editing emerged in the early twentieth century, cinematic storytelling changed altogether. Filmmakers rediscovered what oral and literary storytellers have always intuited and observed. Filmmakers borrowed the conventions of dramatic narrative from literature. In time, many literary writers were drawn to cinematic storytelling techniques.

Dramatic action and the unstoppable passing of time pulse at the heart of good storytelling. Or, put another way, the skillful, thoughtful weaving of scene and summary by turns enriches and textures the narration of any story. All scene and no summary dull a story. The opposite may only hold true for the modern listening reader. For millennia narrators have delivered stories in the grand and sweeping language of summary, letting audiences flesh out details.

When, as a child, I first peeped into the Bible and came upon the first of many staggering genealogies, I sat stunned.

And Cain knew his wife; and she conceived, and bare
Enoch: and he builded a city, and called the name of the
city, after the name of his son, Enoch. And unto Enoch
was born Irad: and Irad begat Mehujael: and Mehujael
begat Methusael: and Methusael begat Lamech. And
Lamech took unto him two wives: the name of the one
was Adah, and the name of the other Zillah. And Adah
bare Jabal: he was the father of such as dwell in tents,
and of such as have cattle. And his brother's name was
Jubal: he was the father of all such as handle the harp
and organ. And Zillah, she also bare Tubalcain, an
instructor of every artificer in brass and iron: and the
sister of Tubalcain was Naamah. (Genesis 4:17–22)

Clearly all summary makes for a generalized narrative,
which is to say a narrative without the kind of drive or
punch or dramatic action that modern readers have come to
treasure, expect, and demand.

To study the evocative power of well-staged scenes
combined with thoughtfully, usefully orchestrated summaries,
I went to look at such fusion in three novels I love.

When poet-novelist N. Scott Momaday's *House Made
of Dawn* went on sale in 1969, I brought this devastating
story home to stay with me awhile. The book has lived on
my shelves ever since. This, his first novel, received the Pulitzer Prize for fiction in 1970. The story still stands as a proto-
type for the native experience in this and other hijacked
lands. Abel, a reservation Indian, a U.S. war veteran—who
will go on trial for stabbing to death an evil spirit, a malevo-
lent albino male witch—decides to try his luck in the world
beyond the reservation. To further thicken his woes, he has
had a closet affair with an unsettling white woman, Angela

Grace St. John. As the luckless Abel moves through this poetically told story, doom closes in around him. Still, he believes in the old tribal ways and beliefs, in the Great Spirit. His people are Bahkyush. The Bahkyush are eagle watchers.

From the book's second section, "The Priest of the Sun," I have picked a portion of a sermon delivered at the Los Angeles Holiness and Pan-Indian Rescue Mission by Reverend J. B. B. Tosamah, Pastor and Priest of the Sun. "The Priest of the Sun," so the story goes, "lived with his disciple Cruz on the first floor of a two-story red-brick building in Los Angeles. The upstairs was maintained by the A. A. Kaul Storage Facility." The basement was "a kind of church, its sacrament peyote." In late January of 1952, Abel goes there with some buddies to hear the Rev. Tosamah preach. "He wore black like a cleric," the novel tells us, "he had the voice of a great dog."

"'*In principio erat Verbum*,'" Tosamah's sermon begins. "Think of Genesis. Think of how it was before the world was made. There was nothing, the Bible says . . . It was dark and there was nothing. There were no mountains, no trees, no rocks, no rivers. There was nothing. But there was darkness all around, and in the darkness something happened. *Something happened!*"

Now let's take a look at a scene from *House Made of Dawn*:

> The axe rang out against her, the incessant sound, hollow, dying away at the source. Once she had seen an animal slap at the water, a badger or a bear. She would have liked to touch the soft muzzle of a bear, the thin black

lips, the great flat head. She would have liked to cup her hand to the wet black snout, to hold for a moment the hot blowing of the bear's life. She went out of the house and sat down on the stone steps of the porch. He was there rearing above the wood . . .

The scene captures exploding moments of sexual connection. We actually see and hear and feel, through symbol and icon, the ripening insides of the guarded and privileged white woman Angela St. John's attraction to Abel, the victimized Indian. Her desire to *know* him in the biblical sense must stay hidden, buried like that wood-chopping axe Abel wields so muscularly. Writers who work on the page enjoy an advantage over writers for the screen; they can slip at once beneath appearance. Novelists and short story writers can needle through the skin of a given character or situation and, in whatever level of language they choose, inject some emotional serum or glue. Angela desires to "touch," "cup," and "hold." Leave it up to the reader to figure out the meaning to Angela of the bear's "wet black snout."

Here's some summary combined with scene from *House Made of Dawn* where the narrator recalls his grandmother's storytelling abilities and how she, unable to read or write, impresses upon her young grandson the transformative power of the spoken word (scene) and the told story (summary):

The white man takes such things as words and literatures for granted, as indeed he must, for nothing in his world is so commonplace. On every side of him there are words by the millions, an unending succession of pamphlets and papers, letters and books, bills and bulletins, commentaries and conversations . . . Consider for a moment that old Kiowa woman, my grandmother, whose use of language was confined to speech . . . for her words were medicine; they were magic and invisible. They came from nothing into sound and meaning. They were beyond price . . . And she never threw words away.

In this section of the novel, Momaday steps up into the bully pulpit and summarizes—perhaps to his own authorial delight—memories, observations, and speculations about language; how it works on paper, how it works when merely spoken with power and sincerity. At a time when most of the people I meet speak twice as quickly as I and my mid-twentieth-century generation did and do, I can't help but understand how drastically the purpose of language itself has changed. Everything happens fast, not quickly. In early films of the twentieth century such transitional summings-up come zooming at us as successive days of newspaper headlines spinning off the printing press, as leaves fluttering from summer-fall-winter-spring dissolves of the same grounded tree, as a hand-holding couple stepping through a first date at the state fair, riding the Ferris wheel, knocking down Kewpie dolls, kissing in the rain. As viewers we get the idea that time is passing and that something significant will come down next. *House Made of Dawn* plays the same game. Abel, nurtured on his grandmother's way with words, will soon see how the white man's manipulation of legal language in a court trial will inevitably bind and chain him yet again.

In *A Lesson Before Dying*, which received the National Book Critics Circle Award for Fiction, Ernest J. Gaines doesn't throw his words away. He tells the story of Grant Wiggins, a brooding schoolteacher who has come back to his little hometown, Bayonne—a plantation, really—in southern Louisiana.

It's the late 1940s. Jackie Robinson has just become the first Negro baseball player to be signed to a contract in the major leagues. Grant realizes that the university education he has, at great sacrifice, gone north to get isn't going to exempt him from the shabby disregard and contempt that whites have always expressed toward blacks in this Cajun town. Cynical, withdrawn, disturbingly self-centered, he can see no way out of, or around, the merciless racism that has practically sentenced him to a kind of solitary self-confinement. Even those with whom he shares love— the godmother who raised him; his aunt; Vivian, a teaching colleague who is also an attractive widow with two young children to raise—even these women can't get Grant to face up to his shrunken heart and shrinking spirit. It isn't until he is drawn into the heroic presence of Jefferson, a slow-witted man wrongfully condemned to death for a murder he did not commit, that Grant begins to understand that there's plenty of pain to go around. The question is: How do you deal meaningfully with such sickness? What can you give of yourself to change or even make a dent in an ignorance so heavily armored that it seems virtually invincible?

Next, part of a scene from *A Lesson Before Dying*:

> I could see the Rainbow Club with its green, yellow, and red arched neon lights. Several cars were parked before the door; one of them, a big white new '48 Cadillac, belonged to Joe Claiborne, who owned the place. A man and a woman came through the door as I got out of my car to go inside. There were probably a dozen people in the place, half of them at the bar, the rest of them sitting at tables with white tablecloths ... The tables in the café had checkered red and white tablecloths. Thelma Claiborne was behind the counter. Thelma ran the café, and her husband, Joe, ran the bar. I asked her what she had for supper.
>
> "Smothered chicken, smothered beef-steaks, shrimp, stew" she said.
>
> "Shrimps any good?" I asked Thelma.
>
> "All my food's good," she said.

What Gaines gives us here qualifies for what Jack Kerouac termed a "prose-movie." From the text alone, a film director could easily shoot powerful dramatic footage. To the mind's eye (and ears and nose and taste and sense of touch), however, we are fully present. Not only do we smell and taste the food, we can see and feel the people. The cook Thelma's caring sarcasm sticks with me like the gravied smell of smothered chicken.

Now, some summary from *A Lesson Before Dying*:

With my back to the fence as I watched them,
I remembered when it was I who had swung
that ax and pulled my end of the saw. And
I remembered the others, too—Bill, Jerry,
Claudee, Smitty, Snowball—all the others.
They had chopped wood here, too; then they
were gone. Gone to the fields, to the small
towns, to the cities—where they died. There
was always news coming back to the quarter
about someone who had been killed or sent to
prison for killing someone else . . . And there
were others who did not go anywhere but
simply died slower.

Character-memory and story are inevitably intertwined.
Look anywhere, in any direction, and the stories to be told
overwhelm imagination. Naturally, we can tell this as: *And
then this happened and then that happened and then he
had ten kids by her and then she caught him in bed with
somebody else and then he had to get rid of her or she of
him so she stabbed him and everything went sour and so it
was that the kingdom fell upon dark days.*

You can always blast or trickle a character back into
her or his beaded chain of personal or intimate history, chro-
nology as emotionally experienced. In the passage just cited,
Ernest Gaines lets us know how his main character, his narrator, Wiggins, never accepted the roles culturally laid out
for him to play. Black and Louisiana-born, he somehow got
it into his head that if he could go away and get a good
education, then white people, the power people, would treat
him differently and respect him. They would see he wasn't

like the other "gone" Negroes. Is he one of the ones who was simply dying slowly?

In 1994, E. Annie Proulx's *The Shipping News* was awarded the Pulitzer Prize for fiction. Remarkable for its quirky, pouty, stylized narration, the novel gives us Quoyle, a knotty-minded, bumbling husband and loving father based in upstate New York. After his runaway cheating wife Petal, headed for Florida with her lover, dies in a ludicrous freeway crash, Quoyle discovers she has sold their daughters to sex traffickers.

It's high-crisis time. Long an occupational ne'er-do-well, Quoyle, for his own sake and the sake of his tender girls, is forced to make a big-time move. Agnis, an aunt who loves her nephew Quoyle and her grandnieces, Sunshine and Bunny, convinces Quoyle that the four of them ought to think about taking a look at the old family house in their ancestral Newfoundland. Agnis herself grew up there, even though it's been fifty years since she's seen the little fishing village of Killick-Claw.

Can anyone ever go home again? They undertake the journey. Against odds that become laughably horrendous, they make a life for themselves in this sea-blustery outpost, where Quoyle, pitiably unqualified at first, lands a job as a journalist for the peculiarly sensationalistic *Gammy Bird*. The paper's editor, Jack Buggit, trusts Quoyle to deliver the kinds of stories about boating catastrophes for which its readers hunger. To me Proulx's *The Shipping News* delivers the old quest, adventure, and love motifs with a sweet, raggedy edge.

Notice now how scene and summary merge in *The Shipping News*:

She spoke of the weather with a man in a watch cap. They talked awhile. Someone else reel footing along said, "Rough today, eh?" She worried about Warren, down in the station wagon, tossing up and down. Wouldn't know what to make of it. Never been to sea. Probably thought the world was coming to an end and he all alone, in a strange car. The man in the watch cap said, "Don't worry, dog'll sleep the 'ole way across. That's 'ow dogs are."

The aunt looked out, saw the blue land ahead, her first sight of the island in almost fifty years. Could not help tears.

This passage from *The Shipping News* demonstrates, as you have already noticed, that scene and summary do combine. Every time we choose a word or lay in a period or tabulate a paragraph, we edit. Something gets left out. Fortunately or unfortunately, language works this way: one word at a time. This is why scene seems genuine while summary seems contrived. Bearing in mind that all of it is fiction, that you're including some facts and excluding others, opens the door to the otherwise mysterious nature of literary storytelling. At times you slow down enough to let us see, seemingly up close, how an event is blossoming, blooming, ripening, taking place. At other times, you summarize, compress, contract, then leap or sail forward or backward.

All three of these novels, each of them personal favorites, have been adapted for the screen. Some may wish to have a look at how screenwriters have translated the for-the-page prose of N. Scott Momaday, Ernest J. Gaines, and E. Annie Proulx into movies.

There are matters I didn't pay close attention to back in 1976, while I was still working for Sidney Poitier. But I did notice one afternoon that a corner of his study was stacked with the novels of James Clavell: *King Rat*, *Tai-Pan*, and *Shogun*, Clavell's blockbuster best-seller at that hour.

"So you're a James Clavell fan?" I said.

"Yes," Sidney told me. "Why not? I have every reason to read and keep all his books. Jim wrote and directed *To Sir, With Love*. I learned a lot from him about scriptwriting and directing."

The 1966 British film *To Sir, With Love* had been one of Sidney Poitier's big-grossing films. In it he plays a beginning teacher assigned to a tough, troubled London high school. Ten years previously, in *Blackboard Jungle*, he had played the hoodlum student. Now he had become the teacher who wins over his unruly pupils by teaching them self-respect. From time to time, the title song—pure lyric summary, recorded by the Scottish singer Lulu—still sneaks into my music-packed, poet-novelist's head. That seems to be the great trick for the canny fiction writer, offering summary and making it sound like part of the music of a scene.

—*2004*

On False Starts

How Not to Begin a Novel When You Don't
Have One to Write

by Lynn Freed

Soon after my second novel, *Home Ground*, was published, my English agent delivered what turned out to be a near-fatal injunction: "If you want to be taken seriously," he said, "we have to have another novel within a year."

The impact of such a statement changes one's life long before one understands the nature of its power. At the time, the words felt less like a threat than a sort of avuncular caveat. *Home Ground* was actually the third novel I'd written—the second was never published—each taking about two years to finish. So, I thought, I'll just do this one quickly.

Then he said, "What's the next novel about?"

I looked at him with the sort of blank stare of dreams, the exam book open on the desk, and no idea how to proceed. This was far worse than, "What books are you reading?"—a question to which I never seem able to conjure an answer. I was hard-pressed even to describe the novel that had just been published. What was it about? A girl growing up in South Africa in the 1950s and '60s? Yes, but—a girl growing up in a theatrical family in the 1950s and '60s? Not really. (Only much later did it dawn on me that the title of the novel itself, which I had in advance of writing the first sentence, was the real subject of the book—of everything I'd written, in fact, and probably of everything I would ever write. *Home Ground*. It was a novel about belonging, about place and displacement. And if, as someone said, we have only one novel in us, I felt sure I had already written it.)

As to a new novel—well, I had no ideas. I had no *need* really, no real desire to write anything. Not for the moment. Not ever, perhaps.

"I think I'll write a sequel," I said.

He recrossed his legs and gave one of those smiling grimaces at which the English are so practiced. "Oh no, no, no," he said, "not a sequel, please."

When the novel came out in New York, I had an almost identical conversation with my New York editor. "We need another book soon," she said. "It's been far too long." And then, "What's it to be?"

And that's when the "what next?" nightmare began.

Every time I start a novel—or a story—for which I am not ready, for which there is not the sort of frisson of conquest that comes with the foot placed surely on familiar territory—I have to learn again what I know already: fiction does not come out of ideas. The sources of fiction are myriad and complex—a character, a character in a situation, a phrase, a scene, a setting, a smell—anything at all but an idea attached to an intention. To bring a story to life, one must inhabit the territory of that story—one must *colonize*—not ring the front doorbell and wait to be let in.

When I sat down to begin the new novel—which, according to the English agent's schedule, should already have been in first draft—all I had in the way of a beginning was a place. It was a bungalow situated on the northeast coast of South Africa, high above the Indian Ocean. I had gone there once as a girl in school. The place belonged to the family of one of the other girls in my class. They used it on weekends and for holidays. We were all taken out there by bus, on a botany expedition to see a mangrove swamp near a lagoon, and then we were to have lunch at the bungalow.

I have forgotten whose bungalow it was. I have forgotten everything about that trip but the gestalt of that wonderful dilapidated bungalow itself and the sight of the sea from its front verandah. Even then, however—although I did not grasp it as such at the time—there was the sure knowledge that this was an Africa more real than any I had experienced in my eleven or twelve years of growing up.

I didn't go back there again, and over the years—both before I left South Africa and during the many visits I've made since—I have driven past the area where I know the bungalow must have been, but have never found it. There is no turnoff through the thick coastal bush, not even the hint of a driveway. I have walked the beaches around there too. Nothing.

But, in the end, it hasn't mattered. Another visit to the place could not possibly have made it more real than it had already become, and, quite possibly, it could have limited the usefulness by tying me down to specifics. I often find— and not only for the purposes of fiction, but for those of all sorts of writing, especially travel essays—that a virgin visit, a purposeless visit, leaves one open to the magic of a place. In this case, and over the years since seeing it, the bungalow became mine more surely than if I owned it myself.

How, after all, *does* one own such a place? How does one own any place? By buying it? By building on it? By happening to have grown up in it? No. And not by loving it either. For the purposes of the imagination, one can only own such a place the way one owns one's own history: by experiencing it, by forgetting it, by re-creating it.

When I came to start the new novel, all I had to start it with was the re-creation of this bungalow, and an idea for a character who had landed up there somehow, felt at home there for the first time in her life. Who she was, however, and why she had come there, I didn't know.

And that's when the nightmare began.

First I decided to give the bungalow to the protagonist's family and have her inherit it from her father. I called her Anna Diamond and wrote in the first person. The novel had no title. This is how it began:

I stood at the edge of the verandah watching the sky blacken into an afternoon storm. The waves, coming in high with the late spring tide, roared out of sight two hundred feet below. The river too ran strong for the time of year. Its dark water traced a cloud of brown almost a mile into the sea.

"Some cup of tea, Miss Annie?"

Well, this was all very well—I was fine as long as I was describing the bungalow. But, try as I might, I could not believe that Anna Diamond's was the sort of family who would own such a place. They were urban people, people who wouldn't venture out into the bush unless they were visiting others like themselves. They were not lovers of Africa; they were sort of temporary sojourners for a few generations. That was the whole point. I needed a *reason*, I was *mad* to find a reason.

So, I came up with a mad sister, who had been banished to the bungalow with her nurse while she was growing up. That is how the bungalow would have come to be in the family. I called the novel *Winter in July*, a play on the reversal of the seasons in the southern hemisphere. Here's how it began:

For the twenty years since my sister Josephine left, the bungalow had stood empty. But now, with my father's death, it was mine. And still it seemed beyond the reach of normal life and rules.

I stood at the edge of the verandah watching the sky blacken into an afternoon storm. The waves, coming in high . . .

But soon I found myself wound up in the sister's madness, explaining and explaining in order to give authenticity to a place that was proving fairly intractable. It kept shrugging off my pathetic attempts to colonize it. And anyway, it wasn't a novel about a mad person; it was a novel about a woman called Anna Diamond, who had come back to South Africa and had landed, somehow—although not this how—at the bungalow. The bungalow stood, the story faltered.

I tried her in the third person.

Anna Diamond stood at the edge of the verandah, watching the African sky blacken into an afternoon storm. The waves, coming in high . . .

Fine as far as it went. But first person/third person was not the problem. As soon as I tried to move the story on from the bungalow, I dried up. I became convinced that, until I solved this very basic problem—*who* was in the bungalow and why—I couldn't go on. (In fact, I couldn't. Fiction has an odd way of both failing the tentative and resisting hot pursuit. Imposing solutions falls under the latter category.)

So I decided to bring Anna Diamond back to South Africa from the United States and place her boldly in the bungalow, to hell with it:

The first real choice Anna Diamond ever made was to return to Africa. She made the choice alone. She made it unconditionally. And she made it against the advice of everyone she knew.

Until then, she'd shown no talent for choosing, for giving up one thing against another. Or for knowing her own mind and heart. What was there to know? Despite her boldness of thought, her head had always hesitated between safety and daring. Except for its primitive leaps of hope, her heart lay still and waiting.

Anna stood at the edge of the verandah, watching the African sky blacken into an afternoon storm. The waves, coming in high . . .

All very well, there she was. I went on with this for a chapter or two, and even gave them as readings. This was a mistake. People would come up to me afterwards and ask, "When will the book be out?" or "Dying to know what happens."

Well, so was I. But I knew enough not to say so. Those questions, however natural and welcome when a book is actually written, simply gave voice and substance to the torment I was in.

What *was* this novel actually about? However much I wrote and rewrote the opening descriptions of the bungalow—the writing itself was never the problem with this novel; the writing itself seldom is—however sure-footed I may have felt about the place, I was timid with the story, with the characters. I didn't *know* this woman, I didn't know the people she had come back to. Worse still, I couldn't *want* to write her story. "Who cares?" I kept asking myself—a deadly question in fiction. The answer was—the answer always is when one has to ask it—no one.

I was becoming desperate. I kept changing the title. The right title, I hoped, might pull the story behind it. Here is what I came up with:

Foreign Territory, In a Foreign Land, Resident Alien, Close to Home, Stranger in a Strange Land, Some Time Overseas, Equal Strangers, Time and Distance, A Way of Life, Voluntary Exile, Far from Home, Overseas Visitor.

Of course, it was hopeless. Still, I chased on. I thought that if only I had the *idea* for the story, I'd have the novel itself. I forgot everything I knew about ideas and fiction. But desperation and vanity do this to a writer: they make her stupid. In fact, finding an *idea* for a novel is easy. I came up with one idea after another. In this case, coming up with an idea for the book was almost a guarantee that whatever I wrote to fit that idea would falter. The more obsessed I became with chasing down a plan, with wrestling the novel into the confines of an abstraction, the more the real fiction eluded me. Nancy Willard once wrote, "A writer with a fixed idea is like a goose laying a stone." I was that goose; I was a flock of such geese.

Several times, I threw the book out and decided that that was it, I would not willingly and knowingly play Sisyphus with fiction. I would write essays, I would write short stories. To hell with agents and editors. I had written forty pages in two years and hadn't got beyond a woman standing on the verandah of a bungalow, looking out over the sea. I'd leave her behind.

But I've never been good at putting failures behind me, certainly not half-baked ones. I am too compulsive, too tidy. To abandon hope for an unpublished novel—such as my second, which I'd written and sent off—this is not the same as abandoning a novel that has yet to take shape, and that, somehow, feels as if there's a shape it can take if only you could find it. The problem was that my imagination, or what was left of it after the battery of intention and ambition, was in revolt. Or in retreat. Anyway, it had left home.

At about this time, I read a review written by Madeleine L'Engle, in which she reported saying to her students, "Don't think. Write. We think before we write a story, and afterward, but during the writing we listen."

This was exactly the problem I was having. I had deafened myself with thinking. The way I write best is in scenes, scenes built upon scenes. But, in this novel, the scenes didn't tie together. My protagonist didn't belong where I had put her. And, anyway, who was she? I had no idea. Under the weight of my anxiety, the novel would no sooner struggle to the surface than it would sink, surface, then sink. There was nothing below the water to hold it up, no four-fifths of the iceberg. I knew that, but I didn't know how to solve the problem.

Somerset Maugham once said, "What I want to feel is that it's not a story I'm reading, but a life I'm living." One can as easily apply this to the writing of a story. To get the story right, one must feel that one is *living* a life rather than writing it. And this is precisely what I could not do.

The question I ask myself now is, What *should* I have done? Should I have let the thing marinate, as I have so often advised others to do, or should I have pushed on, as I did, through four or five miserable years, trying to get it right? I don't know, I can't know.

But I did push on. My protagonist returned to teach for a semester at the university. Then she returned to *look after* her mad sister. Her name changed from Anna Diamond to Joanna Stern. The novel was now called *Halfway to India*.

Joanna Stern stood at the edge of the verandah watching the sky blacken into an afternoon storm. The waves, coming in high with the late spring tide . . .

I could have known that changing a name changes nothing. Nor does changing a title if the fiction isn't there to start with. Still, I changed the title to *Equal Distance* and then to *Pride of Place*. The fact is that fiction hasn't a chance to breathe under the weight of publishing anxieties, or life anxieties. It should ride them out, not carry them on its back.

Sometime in the middle of this awful period, I had a dream, which I wrote down. Here it is:

I went to live with an elephant, a rather fractious one. I made clothes for it. At first its trainer, who was a sort of concierge, thought I wouldn't be able to handle the animal. But, in fact, the elephant and I became quite fond of each other, used to each other. The place in which the elephant lived was a castle, or a prison on top of a mountain, and shaped like an elephant's quarters in the zoo. No one else could handle this elephant, but the keeper seemed to assume I could.

The dream wasn't difficult to work out. In itself, it told me nothing that I did not know. But, having had it, a wonderful thing happened. I gave up. So did my agents, so did my editors. They assumed I was a one-book author (the first book didn't count; it hadn't been noticed enough). Not that they had been nagging me for the book—they hadn't—but that I had felt the weight of expectation in questions like "How's the novel going?" "Anything to show me?" All that stopped.

I decided to write magazine pieces, to do a bit of traveling. I went to the Middle East, down the Nile, through southern Africa and South America. I sold a house and bought a house. The sky didn't fall in. It never seems to do so when one is looking up.

And then, one summer, I was invited by the Rockefeller Foundation to spend five weeks at the Bellagio Study Center on Lake Como. In my proposal I had written four words: "A book of fiction." And now here was the challenge again: make good, come through, try again.

My room and study at the Villa Serbelloni looked out over beautiful terraced gardens and vineyards, over the church towers and terra-cotta houses of Bellagio, and then, beyond that, over Lake Como itself. I had French doors leading out onto a little balcony, a glass-topped desk with a ream of 100 percent rag bond, beautiful pens and pencils, a pencil sharpener, an eraser, a notebook—all new, all wonderfully Italian. But where was the computer I'd been told would be mine for the visit? I went downstairs to inquire.

There'd been a hitch, I was told. In that charming Mediterranean way of the Italians, I was told that someone's spouse had wanted a computer, and now she would be using it until she left, another two weeks. Meanwhile, I could print out whatever I had on my disks; I could write in the notebook, would that help?

I decided to take a walk down to the lake for coffee, three-hundred-odd steps down, a double espresso and a look in the shops, three hundred steps up again. By the time I was back in my study, the panic was manageable. I sat down. I took up one of the pencils, opened the notebook, and wrote, "Untitled." Then I had to lie down on the bed and sleep for the rest of the day.

I'd written my first two novels with pencil and paper, written them in a flash through one draft, typed it out, cut and pasted and rewritten. But now the ease of editing-as-you-go on a computer had changed my way of working completely. I tried hard to remember how I'd done it.

After breakfast the next morning, I printed out the twenty-five false drafts I had on my disk, took them back up to my study, and read them through. I also read through the file of notes I'd brought. And then I put them all in an envelope and put them away in my suitcase. I opened the notebook, underlined "Untitled," and began to write.

I like to think that the pencil and paper themselves were responsible for the ease with which I now wrote—the simple, laborious, almost nostalgic act of fashioning words by hand. As I was writing the new opening, I even seemed to be hearing the words differently, fake from real. Hearing the story too. And, once I did, I knew quite clearly who my protagonist was. What was all the fuss about? My Anna Diamond, my Joanna Stern, my many-named, variously described protagonist, with her disparate reasons for inhabiting a bungalow on the coast of southern Africa, was really Ruth Frank, the narrator of *Home Ground*, grown up now and sobered. And whatever the editors said they didn't want from me, what *I* wanted was to write a sequel. And that was what I was doing.

From that point on, I had no trouble with the novel. I knew my character, and I knew why she had come back.

Here is how I wrote the new beginning:

Even though it is a commonplace among expatriates that one might miss the death of a parent—even though, in fact, my father hadn't died at all; hadn't, perhaps, even had a heart attack, just a fright—I came to understand, when I finally did get home, that my absence had become a part of the family drama.

Ruth Frank had come back to attend the apparent death of a parent, yes, and she would go to the bungalow, certainly, but it wouldn't be *her* bungalow at all. It would belong to her first lover, a lover that she had left behind eleven years before, and with whom she would take up again. The lover, Hugh Stillington, would come from the sort of family from which the girl in my class at school had come—old colonial, old sugar money.

The first time Hugh Stillington had brought me out to the bungalow, I hadn't been ready for his world. I'd sat on the verandah thinking of things to say as he'd dismissed the servants in a perfect Zulu and then poured me a sherry from an old cut-glass decanter . . .

Hugh Stillington was a lost cause—an eccentric, who carried on at his Africans about crop rotation and eating fish when he should have been running for Parliament. He'd given up, she said, given in to the old-fashioned seduction of land and people. Which was all very well for him—his sons had been in England for fifteen years. Bloody aliens! Hugh had roared. Comfortable, like their mother, in cold, damp, noisy places. He wouldn't have them back.

With this I felt at home. I wrote on. I moved the novel from the 40 pages with which I had been obsessing—and which I had now rewritten entirely—to 100, 250, 350. This is not to say that the process was easy—I'd be stuck here or there, of course, and think, "This is it, here I go again"—but in the main I knew what I was doing. The territory was my own, its characters, its story. It was a novel about place and displacement, *plus ça change, plus c'est la même chose*.

The day I finished the novel, I still didn't have a title. None of the titles I had used seemed right. I had put them in and taken them out one after another until I started writing properly. And then I forgot about a title and all the superstitions that go along with it. But now I had finished; I needed one.

A friend was coming for dinner, and I asked her for suggestions.

"But what's it about?" she said.

I told her. I gave her the manuscript. She opened it here, opened it there at random.

"What is this bungalow?" she asked.

I told her.

"So, call it *The Bungalow*," she said.

And there it was. I sent the manuscript to my New York editor. She gave me some notes for a rewrite—leave out one of the sisters, she said, and a few of the scenes, and, by the way, you have far too many dogs in this novel. I cut out the sister (a big mistake, as it turned out) and put a few more dogs in for good measure. And then I delivered the final manuscript myself, on a trip to New York. The publisher called me in a few days later. "Lynn," he said, "you have thrown away a big novel here. You have a black man murdering a white man—why didn't you put it up front?"

"But that's not at all what the novel is about," I said.

"What is it about then?" he asked.

I gave him the place and displacement speech. He looked skeptical. "Put the murder up front," he said, "and we'll publish it."

It was a deal. And away I went to write a new beginning. *She married him in cold blood. Stunningly ugly she was . . .*

Perhaps if I had actually seen his body after the murder—brains and blood, the nostrils slit to ribbons, one eye out of its socket [I invent these things; all I know is "stabbed"]—perhaps then I would have felt the loss more violently.

I didn't mind in the least. I knew I could write a new scene for the front of the book without changing the nature or the point of the novel. In fact, I could use the scene to tie things up, front and back. And I could still have my protagonist standing on that bloody verandah, looking out at the sea—which now came later anyway—using all my old phrases, and images, polished to a gloss over five years of rewriting. The point is that I knew why she was there, I knew her. I'd written the book.

—1999

A Note to an Unpublished Writer

by Louis B. Jones

Of course, publication is supposed to be the goal; and of course, at all times, you have to believe or pretend publication is important; but years later the solid books on the shelf will turn out to be only an accumulated by-product and a necessary accident of a more important, mysterious process, a process going on outside the writer's skin as well as inside. There are writers out there everywhere, published and unpublished, generating heaps of paper, and we're all making big mistakes—mistakenness being our métier, infinite mistakes being the atoms we build from. But one or two will be polishing their personal mistake until it shines like a blade. In the darkness you must work in, beware of what looks like success looming up shining its search lamp; and in case publication does come along, if you're lucky you'll get away fast from that strobe-photographed picture of your work, because you'll have fresh work and will already be far ahead in obscurity. Which is where you are now.

By "mistake" I suppose I mean the artistic risk that looks merely erroneous before it becomes acknowledged (in the marketplace) as having been necessary. Any of the wonderful books you might think of are composed of their inevitable defects. Look at the ennui of *Moby-Dick* or the difficulty of Emily Dickinson, or James's clotted prose style, Twain's tiresome clowning and cutting for the gag, Austen's restriction to parlors and marriages, Updike's addiction to language, Proust's insistence on examining every last thing. We forgive the work its weaknesses because the weaknesses themselves mount steeply up toward the one great page we're there reading for. Look how "mistaken" Thoreau's *Walden* or Dickens's *Bleak House* or Joyce's *Ulysses* still are. Certain books, in order to get at something else, risked a boredom or a vulgarity or a peculiarity which today we overlook. Or which we consider their exact triumph.

The wonderful thing literature can do is license peculiarity itself: it can actually make our real world brighter, and warmer, by naming something we'd always half-known but never felt fully entitled to. It announces, very quietly and intimately, the censored thought, the eccentric conviction. In that way it makes our lives more familiar to us, more useful to us. (Lives that ought to have been utterly familiar and useful already, since they are *ours*.) The printed page brings two remote strangers, reader and writer, in contact. No event in civilization is more important, or more intimate, than this contact—this contact right here now—between a writer and a reader, who at all other waking hours of the rational day appear to be two separate people.

The special advantage of literature is that it doesn't (like the movies, say, or like people) dodge around and make a lot of noise and then vanish from view: literature, on paper in dried-ink marks, is made of assertions that stay put, fairly to be examined, lying open to the play of the eye.

Sentences committed to paper risk outlasting the decades' intellectual fads (fads that, you notice, even the mass of *smart* people, the very most admired people, for an epoch, can get sucked into).

Instead, the disembodied voice of the author says, I'm alone in a room transcendent of history; you're alone now too; or if anyone is there with you, erase them from your ear. Of course, you must build "my" story only out of your own ideas and experiences. So in this mirror of a shared sentence, recognition takes place: the actual "writing" turns out to be, wholly or in part, the reader's job: the reader actively writes each sentence as he goes; this little fountain of words rises within *your* brain stem. Its substance is provided by *your* reflection and experience. The miracle of the grammatical sentence is that it can be shared—that it can thump softly through the wall of the lonely self.

Ah, but gentle reader, what intervenes between us. It's this awkward noisy event called publication, and it threatens to make impostors of us both. First, ignore the dust jacket; that's the work of an artist in a Midtown cubicle with a drafting board; take the dust jacket off and throw it away, to reveal the plain coffin that a book properly is. Pay no attention to my snotty voice on NPR, and don't flip to the author photo in case there's one reproduced in the front matter. All those photos of Authors—wolf-faced Authors, goose-faced Authors, cat-faced, horse-faced, alligator-faced, or gerbil-faced, their hair by photographers' stylists slicked back or fluffed up, their collars petted down nicely or raised rakishly—endanger the more important *recognition* that's possible between reader and writer. The recognition I'm looking for is, as you might encounter a bank teller or a ticket vendor, only a practical momentary gaze through the page, strictly impersonal and polite. Children with a mirror like to play a scary game: you sit alone with the glass and stare at your own image and let your features go slack so your face is emptied of all personality. Suddenly, without any protection of the usual amiable mask, it's a total stranger in there. Monstrously, it's "the other," right there before you.

What effigies all human experience is made of! Take two figures opposed at history's moral extremes: the exemplary Jew and the exemplary Nazi. How, across the division of a strand of barbed wire, do they "recognize" each other? How do they "identify" each other? How does the Nazi "know" the Jew, or the Jew "know" the Nazi? By reaching inward. They look inside themselves, to see the other. Martin Buber and Hermann Goering, by grace of literature, may converse within this eternal room, this library above history, this room you're in when you write. It's the same room you're in when you read. It's the room where Nietzsche talks with Socrates or with Camille Paglia, where Sylvia Plath converses with Julius Caesar and Woody Guthrie, Freud with Keynes, Karl Marx with Bob Dylan, Charles Darwin with St. Paul. In this ideal, polite room, a conversation between a Jew and a Nazi is made possible by mutual recognition. The one is simply able to "identify" the other. The word comes from *idem*, meaning "same" in Latin; and its modern use in the phrase "identify with" is germane. If they're going to recognize each, across the historical strand of barbed wire, the Nazi and the Jew must "same-ify" or "equate" themselves each with the other, discovering the other in himself.

Because in life our bodies are separate, we fall naturally into the theatrical convention that our souls are separate, separate ghosts. I used to make a habit of writing every morning in a suburban donut shop on a mall, where one day the shy, polite, limping El Salvadoran janitor touched glances with the blonde in her polka-dot skirt who, every morning, double-parked her 450SL and picked up a roll and coffee to go. I remember the moment. They crossed each other's paths, and for a moment had to negotiate space sharing. His mop handle slanting between them like a cancellation sign, their gazes touched, across a distance of, oh, three feet on the linoleum. It's unlikely that anything flirtatious was exchanged in the glance, though they were both of an eligible age. It was just a two-second period when each had to acknowledge the other's existence. And when that eye contact was made, infinite assumptions ramified everywhere throughout the universe. Alliances of love and money were defined, pledges of class and beauty and race. Each stood at the very tip of a separate history, but then suddenly a *shared* history. And all those assumptions were informed by his and her literacy in this culture. Their lives are determined by the conversation in that civilized room above history. It's a very real conversation, and its consequences are all around us.

Now let me bring all this back to the topic of publication and the book business. Impatience is an increasingly important force in our time, especially where profit is an avowed motive, and impatience can be a not-altogether-good influence on the course of things. Reviewers are expected to give immediate responses to a book. Publishers watch for the first spike of sales. Editors, to keep their jobs, have to be able to point to successes, recent successes, which will be defined by profit figures. Additionally, a great number of writers want to get into the rich-and-famous category, and so that becomes a motive widely considered legitimate. Altogether, it's a chain of motives that produces a certain kind of book. At the receiving end of this publication process, standing out there on the mall in front of an eye-catching cardboard "book dump" display, is the under-estimated reader, distrustful of hype, self-distrustful too, but reaching for his wallet.

But fortunately, a book is a mysterious artifact, its original motives dark, its future consequences unplannable. The saving irony of the publisher's art is that the books are never really "understood," not by anybody, not even by their writers truly, or by their agents or editors or publicists, or by the keenest reviewers, or even by their most loving readers. We're all handling a magical substance here, which can spring into fire on our hands. In the publishing biz, big deals turn out to be duds. Duds turn out to be big deals. Under the lights, the text is a changed thing. Its errors and accidents grow to rescue it. Or, its sleek perfections stamp it with mediocrity. Getting published can make a writer start to feel like a deconstructionist: she sees her book go off into the world and lead a very independent life she'd never intended, sprout wings or hoofs.

The point here—and I intend this as a reason for faith—is that when in our obscurity we work, we're stitch-ing within a double-sided tapestry: our personal mistakes are our medium. All we have to do is keep our heads down at the workbench. At one point when my first novel was coming out, I stood in a Miami bookstore beside a stack of my books, and I was wearing on my lapel an immense blue ribbon, like the ribbon awarded the prize pig at a county fair, as big as a sunflower, with a ruffled central disk, stamped in gold letters "AUTHOR." (In the book-publicity business, helpful, enthusiastic people have ideas like these, which the fond first-time author goes along with.) Wearing that decoration, I was ignored by passersby on the mall, or else regarded warily so people veered to avoid me. My face had appeared in at least ten American newspapers that week. And it occurred to me then, as I stood there wearing a blue ribbon half as big as my face, that what a writer really wants is to imitate Shakespeare and be dead already.

I know, there are writers who do want to stand *in front of* their own book; they're good at it, and they plainly delight their readers, or at least their readers don't seem to be excessively critical of such a writer's accumulated pages after they've read them. Beside me was a stack of my handsome-looking hardcovers—priced so that a minimum-wage burger-flipper would have to work four hours to pay for a single volume—and my mind escaped forward to the year 2000-something, when that same novel, in a used paperback edition, might lie on a card table at a garage sale. I picture it as a paperback out of fashion in its cover illustration, dented at the corners and flaking at the spine, sold for ten cents to a girl who recognizes its title from some friend's parents' bookshelf; or maybe to a fifteen-year-old boy who is first attracted by a *misunderstanding* of the title, a misunderstanding all his own; and he'll take it home to be alone with it for hours, in that peculiarly intense, vital solitude of the reader. He'll be alone with "the author," but really he'll be alone with himself, great unexplored canyons of himself, so I may hope.

And that will be the most honorific form of publication. That is the author's glory. I myself won't be standing by as the book's nervous angel. No publicity or advertising will have urged him to esteem the book. And, not least important, no one of us in this business will get a penny off that transaction. Whatever merit remains in the book will have reverted to its original "gift" status, reborn hype-free, and free of the author's original intention. Who knows, that young reader may even mistrust his own peculiar esteem for my novel. Even the most scrupulous readers can't immediately feel all the results of a novel in themselves. Years afterward, some book that, at the time, they may have consciously disliked comes back to them with that gift. An old man on a park bench, say, gets an idea that the best thing he ever did was, one summer, be patient and read even the boring parts of Proust.

I have a friend who is the main editor at one of the huge New York houses, and he told me over the telephone, in almost a whining tone, "People think books should be 'mainstream.' They're just not. Occasionally a *Da Vinci Code* comes along, and for a minute, it seems like the entertainment conglomerates got their wish and books are a mainstream commodity. But they're basically outside the mainstream." On the phone he let his voice rise. "We want to be *surprised*," he grieved, speaking on behalf of the whole book business.

So in benediction I want to wish you many years of unsettledness and uncertainty. Stay hungry. Suspect all your own successes and comforts and complacencies. Keep getting your feelings hurt. If the very editor or agent who pleads *We want to be surprised* rejects your work, well, then the hell with him. You can take your business right down the street. New York is a big town. It's not like our small towns in the West. It's big enough to host anarchy. That's the whole point of New York. It's a market. It's a brokerage. So when you say "I'm taking my business right down the street," there are plenty of streets in New York you can be referring to.

And choose your reader well. Somebody you can respect. Don't imagine a reader beneath you, as so many writers seem to, because, in your immortality, you're going to be stuck with this person. This is going to have been your best labor, so don't squander it. Just think of all this work you do! Your mind wanders to your fictional characters while you're talking to a real person. You bolt your food at dinner. Your extremities are cold. You can't even enjoy something simple like a movie anymore. Your wife is disgusted with the way you've started sleeping with your boots on, embracing your shovel, at the bottom of the hole you've dug so far. In the flowerpot on the railing outside, the cylinder of dirt has shrunk to a white can. The waste of the writer's life is patent everywhere, in the obvious fact of total, immediate, universal misunderstanding and oblivion.

But at the same time, oblivion is the writer's special privilege and power: she (or he) exists in a fortunate state of infinite obscurity moving over the face of the waters. Within that dark purity is all the necessary intimacy. Pity rather the well-published writer, who by contrast has enemies among his friends: people who "understand" him! The closer they are, the greater is the danger of their understanding. Perhaps he even starts thinking he understands himself, and then he's his own worst enemy. I won't name any names, but just think of how many good writers' fate was, after a great book or two, such statuary petrifaction.

Because writing is luckiest when, right there on your worktable, it's crumbling in stages of disintegration and unruliness. Only when the writer is rising through a series of his own misunderstandings is he achieving the necessary self-transcendence, making the necessary mistake. The writer's paltry original intention turns out to be insufficient to the great mysterious laws of fiction, like the laws of astrology and physics all around him in the dark as he swims. He is flung out there with nothing but his impoverished imagination, an old blue flannel drawstring bag containing a few saved objects, a stone, a feather, a broken clothespin, a whistle, a pebble of Play-Doh, the same old things. That blessed impoverishment, the bottom of the barrel when you hit it, is precisely the cornucopia you wished for. We are all so utterly ignorant about the life going on all around us. A writer spends most of his time "off the trail," crashing among thickets. And so the writer (by nature a highly organized person, disdainful of people who get lost or people who don't have a plan) finds himself lost. Maybe you have to believe, like the Protestants, that the best happiness for mortals is in hard work alone, the fruit of that work merely a snare and a pitfall.

By which I mean publication, I suppose. A snare and a pitfall. I'm directing these remarks to the most ambitious writer, not the mere fulfiller of people's expectations, who may get published more easily, and may even be disgusted by the heroism and vanity of this portrait of a job. Such a writer will have stopped reading many pages ago. So it's just us here now, pulling into the stretch, and it's safe to talk.

To the one or two who want to give rather than take, I just want to say: Have a little faith. And let faith chasten you. It's no mere metaphor; there really is an encounter in Valhalla between Bob Dylan and St. Paul. It's a consequential conversation. And there really will be an actual boy buying a used book at a garage sale, and he's an extremely important person. He doesn't know quite how to inhabit the world yet, what to do with it all, what to do with himself. And he actually will pause with his finger on a title, in all the boredom and moral lull of a Midwestern August.

It's Wilmette. The garage sale is in the shady alley by Fourth and Greenleaf. The cicadas are singing in the elms. I begin to see what I've written. The El train can be heard in the distance gathering speed as it departs, racketing away toward Chicago. It's been you all along, with whom I'll spend eternity. Well, this then is a promise—though in your lostness and your anger, you may not recognize it— this is a promise I can send straight back to you. Publication is desirable, but you've already got what you will most desire: work. You're already in the very middle of all the work you could want. You're already in that ideal afterlife. The later, rather funerary event of publication—seeing your own words come back at you typeset as if someone else had written them—will be educational, a command, a kick. But then you will want to put that behind you right away. You will want to recover the obscurity you swim best through. You've got eternal youth there. You'll never be satisfied. If you get lucky, it will be a darkness so pure it will mirror not the "self," but the mysterious "other."

—*1996*

FEAR OF FINISHING

by Mark Childress

I have a friend I'll call Buddy. He and I started writing our first novels the same year, 1979. Actually, I had written a *first* first novel in high school, which I have never showed to anybody because I am embarrassed by it. I am not sure if I am embarrassed because it is heavingly, hysterically bad or because it is the best thing I ever wrote.

It had to do with these very Carson McCullers–y people, all cripples and mutes and dwarfs living in these broken-down old houses in a dusty God-haunted ruined Alabama town. I don't know if any of the characters had a job, but they all had pellagra or scabies or rickets or something, and I know it was very hot all the time. It was August all the time in that book. There was a lot of intense staring—at the ceiling, at the walls—God, there were a lot of ceiling fans in that book. And old rattly table fans that turned their faces from side to side. There was a great deal of very intense interior adverby monologue of a fevered and watery adolescent sort. "He looked ruinously across the kudzu-choked field toward the fantastically shabby sharecropper shack and thought about how life is one big unhappy shower of pain."

Like that. I hate to think how bad it probably was, but then again I also hate thinking that it might have been my high-water mark as a writer.

I remember my mute, deformed dwarfs lying about on their vine-clotted porches, drinking exotic cocktails I named out of the back of Mom's Betty Crocker cookbook, the section on entertaining: Grasshoppers, Singapore Slings, Harvey Wallbangers, Fuzzy Navels. At the time I had never tasted alcohol—closest I ever came was the watered-down Welch's grape juice at Presbyterian communion—but I imagined how a cocktail would taste, and I was sure that all sophisticated characters drank them. I thought my novel might be just bohemian and weird enough to be published. I was aware that Truman Capote published his first book when he was seventeen, only a year older than I. Time was a-wastin'.

And you know what? For all I know, it may have been good enough to be published. I'll never know. I never finished it. I got within fifty pages of the end, and stopped.

I believe that was a mercy, but I can't be sure.

For all I know, it's the worst book ever written.

For all I know, it's the best book I'll ever write.

And the thing is, I'll never know. Because I'll never finish that book. And I'll never show it to anybody.

But oddly enough, I haven't burned the manuscript. I have had plenty of opportunities. I guess since it's unfinished, some part of me is still considering the possibilities.

In some ways, that book is my favorite of all my books. Because it's not done. Not finishing a book can be so much more satisfying than finishing. Just stop. Before it's done. Let the ending be implied. Let it live in a drawer, forever.

If you never get around to finishing it, see, it's still a great book. It will always be a potentially great book. It has unlimited potential. It might win you the Nobel Prize in literature, all by itself.

If you finish it, and especially if you publish it, chances are you will find out how great it was not.

This is a secret most writers share. We are loath to begin a new book because we know that, ONE, we will never be able to write the book we have in mind, and, TWO, before we know it the book will be harassing us to finish it. You can be ten pages into the book and you're already wondering, Oh how the hell am I ever going to END this damn thing? You can be writing the first sentence and some voice inside you is already saying, I AM NEVER GOING TO FINISH THIS FREAKING BOOK.

Inside the world of the novel, when you are living in there, it's kind of a wonderful but sublimely lost place to be. Things happen slowly—at least in my books. . . . Life happens in very slow motion as you accrete the details, one upon the other. It may be a scene that takes thirty seconds to read, and it may cover two minutes in novel-time, and those two minutes may take two months to write.

Life comes to life, one tile at a time, one snatch of dialogue taking shape, then another, then a bit of time passing, some detail of nature, then a look around the book for whichever of the characters we might have forgotten and need to weave back in. Each chapter becomes a room you live in for a while, two weeks or eight weeks or twelve weeks or two years, however long it takes. You live in that one room obsessively. You run your fingers over every inch of the furniture, stitching in by hand every intricate loop of the carpeting. You hang the chandelier one crystal at a time, refining it as you go along, redesigning. You repaint the room every time you come into it. You run your fingers over the back of the sofa, down the wallpaper, to the light switch. You flip the lamps on and off. You burn incense in that room, trying to get the earlier smell out.

Sometimes it's hard to leave that room. You get to liking that sofa. The chintz becomes comforting in the regularity of its pattern. Even if you hate chintz, its pattern gives you comfort.

The point I keep coming back to, as I circle this back around to include my good friend Buddy, who started writing his novel the same year as me, 1979, is that the unwritten novel, in the mind of the novelist who hasn't written it yet, is so far superior a thing to the finished novel—to any finished novel—that it's something of a miracle that any novelist ever finishes a book.

Can you imagine how great Herman Melville thought *Moby-Dick* was going to be when he started? Can't you imagine how he felt when he finally turned it in—"oy vey, that long part about dredging my hands in the milky sperm of the whale, how embarrassing, and as a matter of fact, looking back on it now, the whole thing seems a good deal more homoerotic than I intended."

These are the kinds of things you never come to know, or at least I haven't come to know them yet with any certainty, and I have just finished up novel number six (counting only the ones that eventually I finished, and published). How good or bad it is, is something that you as the writer of it simply cannot know.

Of course, the moment when a book is best comes before you have written a word of it. Let me repeat, a book is at its absolute best—and will never be better—than when it is unwritten. When it's only an idea. A shiny beautiful thing twisting and dangling in midair. A concept, a notion, a radical reinvention of the very idea of the novel. A shade, an arc, a passage of time . . . a big swath of pages easily written, in the naive and simpleminded imagination of the novelist imagining himself in the act of writing it.

After that, it only gets worse. Every page you write is in some ways a tiny death . . . of the illusion with which you began. Every clumsy, unstructured, redundant sentence that you apply to paper is one less deathless, tripping, dancing, rhythmical, internally rhyming piece of brilliance like that you had in mind when you sat down at the piano and started to play.

These people who write a new book every year—the way some people buy a new car—well, it's just disgraceful, if you ask me. Someone who writes a book every year has no fear of finishing, whatsoever. And although I can safely say I aspire to write a sentence as fine as some that John Updike has written, let me also say that the world would be better off if he had had more fear of finishing certain of his books. *Memories of the Ford Administration*, for instance. That would have made a fantastic unfinished novel. I think also of John Irving, whose endings are almost always the strongest portion of his book: think of Owen Meany doing his historic layup shot; think of Garp circling back around to the only possible ending, which was the beginning, which was the sentence, "In the world according to Garp, we're all terminal cases."

So anyway my good friend Buddy was writing this great unfinished novel of his, which he started in 1979, the same time I started my real first novel, *A World Made of Fire*. That book took me four years, working nights and weekends, but finally there were only two possible words left to write, and I wrote them: The End.

I finished a book! Time to celebrate! So why don't I feel like celebrating? Why do I feel like my whole family has just died?

Because, in fact, they have. The whole crowd of imaginary people with whom I have spent the last four years—well, they are all dead. All killed off by me, by those two little words: The End. I will rewrite—oh boy, will I—but I will never again have the experience of living inside that particular world for four years.

The book wasn't anywhere near as good as I thought it would be when I started. They never are, you know. But God I was thrilled, because Knopf published it, and a few reviewers liked it, and it sold about nine copies, seven of which were bought by my mother.

And I thought, not so good if you thought you were writing a best seller, you know, but also not so bad for a first novel, right? You got blurbs from James Dickey and Erskine Caldwell, for God's sake. That's not so bad, right? The whole thing was very hard to do, but surely you've learned something, it'll get easier with the second book.

Guess what? The blank page only gets blanker. It gets blanker the more pages you fill. I have this idea that each of us has a finite number of words that are worth saying . . . I for instance may have 2,345,349 words of fiction in me, and when they're all used up, that's it. OR NOT. If you're as old as ol' Krusty Mailer, let's say, and you've been cranking 'em out every few years your whole adult life, these fantastically long-winded books—and let's face it, Mailer hasn't had anything new to say since shortly after the Nixon administration—you must find each succeeding piece of paper so incredibly blank that it's amazing if you're able to write an e-mail. It's a function of how much you've said—how much of the sum total of everything you have to say you have already inflicted upon your audience—divided by how much linguistic energy you still possess.

So Buddy was writing this novel, see, which he started in 1979, and it had to do with a boy who lives way out in the sticks in south Alabama, and for kicks he likes to dress up in a werewolf suit and go around scaring people.

Buddy kept writing this same book, rewriting it, reinventing it, over and over, for fourteen years.

He finished it. A dozen times. And I misspoke, it was not the same book. Every time he wrote it, it became another book. He did so many completely different drafts that at one time or another that book was about nearly everything. Race, history, gender, the illusion of self, Christian fundamentalism, folklore, the persistence of memory. The Civil War. The civil rights movement. The Brothers Grimm.

It began as a kind of violent folktale, in the vein of Harry Crews or Barry Hannah.

For a while it became a lyrical love story, á la Eudora Welty's *The Robber Bridegroom*.

For a while it was a redneck adventure, something like *Deliverance*.

Then it became a kind of futuristic sci-fi novel about a totalitarian land of religious fanatics, and one lone rebel boy in a werewolf suit.

That was the version he finished. That was the version that got published. An amazing, original book. A book like nobody else ever wrote.

After fourteen years, he had finally exhausted all the possibilities.

In those years, I wrote three novels. I don't know if my three unsatisfactory endings were more satisfying, to me, in sum, than Buddy's one. I think they were probably equally satisfying: the point was not the finishing, but the time we spent writing. Each of my books feels less finished, to me, than the one that came before. I keep trying to unthink the process of writing. In other words, each time I aspire to have less of a plan in mind when I start. You can't help having SOME kind of plan for the end, but too much of a plan, for me, is death. Writing for me is like walking a tightrope into a very dense fog. You have faith that the other end of the rope is tied to something, but damned if you have any idea what, and the whole point of the exercise is to grope your way forward until you find out what is holding you up.

If you start out with a boy in a werewolf suit, you hope he will still be there at the end.

But if not, a novel is endless possibilities, and you'd better finish the one you've started so you can start a new one.

Remember, though, as soon as you start it, you start having to finish it.

My friend Buddy finally published his werewolf book. It was fantastic. A good many reviewers liked it; it sold about nine copies, seven to his mother, and one to my mother, and one to me.

That all happened in 1993. And later that year, he started another novel. He's been writing his second novel for a number of years now. When it started out, it was the story of the last surviving Confederate soldier, who develops an obsessive desire to hunt down and kill the last surviving Yankee soldier in his nursing home in New Hampshire. That's what it was about when it started. Thirteen years ago. We have no idea what it's about these days. We're expecting to see a first draft somewhere midway through the second Clinton presidency. We know it's going to be spectacular.

In other words, writing a novel for me, and for my friend Buddy, is kind of like this week will be for you. Right now, as it begins, the week ahead seems endless. It stretches out before you, a succession of days spent at this strange altitude among this roomful of strangers, each one of whom seems to have about fifteen times as much raw literary talent as you. All these odd-looking people trying not to act nervous. Pretty soon time will stop inching along and it will start to fly. And you'll stay up too late tonight trying to get to know some of these people, and there may be a hot tub involved. Then Monday morning's workshop will seem either fabulous or horrifying, depending upon whether it is your story that is being discussed. Then somewhere around Tuesday time will stop dead completely. Then it will lurch and stumble along, it will halt and fly in a herky-jerky way, and there will be this TEENY-TINY nervous breakdown you'll be having along about Wednesday night or so, and there will be the thing with that fifth glass of red wine and the late-night mixer in that guy's room in the house you don't quite remember where it is—up that hill somewhere. And then by Friday it will seem the week refuses ever, EVER to end, and simultaneously it will feel like time is aboard the Sunset Limited and roaring through the station without stopping. And you will think your head will explode and you might have to kill somebody, possibly including yourself, but more likely including a bunch of random strangers who just happened to get in your way, but through some sort of miraculous intervention that will not come to pass, after all. And then Saturday will be here. THE END, it's over, it's time for you to go home.

Your head will be stuffed full of words. You will have a bunch of confusing and contradictory responses to your work, but by God you WILL get some responses. And though they will not be exactly what maybe you had hoped, and you will not have suddenly become Amy Tan and be trying to decide which publisher's entreaty you will entertain, this will not have happened to you because it didn't happen to Amy either until she had done a lot of hard work. But still those responses, though they are not the answer to your dreams, will be respectful and mostly they will be trying really hard and with all their generosity to understand what the hell it is you are trying to say. And you will discover that there are a lot of people just as odd and uncomfortable as you, and they're called WRITERS, and you are one of them, so all you have to do now is—

Finish it.

Go home and finish it.

Be afraid. Be deathly afraid. Or don't be afraid at all, and just keep typing until you come to the writer's two scariest, two most favoritest words in the world . . .

The end.

—2006

Angst and the Second Book

by Amy Tan

I am glad that I shall never again have to write a Second Book. About two weeks after I turned in the manuscript for *The Joy Luck Club* to Putnam, a friend showed me a book, whose title I've mercifully forgotten, which listed hundreds of major novelists throughout the centuries, with career summaries glimpsed through bar graphs. The graphs, similar to records of annual rainfall amounts, represented the relative critical success of each of the authors' books, a statistical epitaph of sorts. For some, a flood of sudden success—then unrelenting drought, book after book after book.

"Isn't it interesting," my friend noted, "how many writers went on to write lousy second books?"

I never considered that the critics might have been wrong. Instead, I stayed up half the night reading that book, and by morning I had decided that whatever those writers had lacked—confidence, stamina, vision, sharp red pencils—I would stock in extra portions. Each of my books, I determined, would outdo its predecessor, increasing in scope, depth, precision of language, intelligence of form, and thus critical acceptance and perhaps even readership.

Of course, that's what I determined *before* I was published, before *The Joy Luck Club* ever hit the best-seller list, before I attended my first literary luncheon, where a woman asked me with absolute sincerity, "How does it feel to have written your best book first?"

Shortly after the book was published, I was in New York having lunch with my editor, Faith Sale, as well as a friend of hers, another writer, the author of four books. The friend asked me if I had started the Second Book.

"I have some ideas," I said vaguely. I was loath to admit in front of Faith that I had not the slightest idea what I would do next. "I just haven't decided which one to go with," I added. "All I know is that it won't be *Son of Joy Luck*."

"Well, don't sweat over it too much," the other writer said. "The Second Book's doomed no matter what you do. Just get it over with, let the critics bury it, then move on to your third book and don't look back." I saw the bar graphs of my literary career falling over like tombstones.

I was to hear this same doom and gloom, or permutations of it, from many writers. Actually, I cannot recall *any* writer—with or without splashy debut—who said the Second Book came easily. The Second Book is bound to be trashed, one said, especially if the first was an unexpected success. The Second Book is always a disappointment, said another, because now everyone has preformed expectations. Critics will say it is too much like the first. Readers will complain that it is too different.

"It's as though you're always competing against yourself," said one writer friend, whose first book met with unanimous praise, quickly propelling him upward to literary heights. The Second Book was compared with the first and received mixed reviews. The third and fourth earned renewed praise, but the first always managed to creep into reviews as the standard. "You begin to hate the first book," he said. "It's like the kid brother sticking his tongue out, going, 'Nah-nah-nah.'"

"The critics are always worse when the first book was really, really big," confided another writer. "With the first, they put you on this great big pedestal. But by the time the Second Book comes around, you realize you're not sitting on a pedestal at all. It's one of those collapsible chairs above a tank of water at the county fair."

"It's like that Mister Rogers song," said another writer friend, "the one that says, 'You'll never go down, never go down, never go down the drain.' My daughter heard that song. And after that, she started screaming in the bathtub, scared out of her mind she was going to be sucked down the drain. And then the next day I went to speak at a literary luncheon and overheard some people whispering, 'Can she do it again? Can she really do it again?' They put fear in me. They were saying, 'Honey, you *can* go down the drain.'"

Only one person—a reporter on the literary scene—told me not to worry. "The Second Book is *nothing*," he said. "Everyone expects it to be weaker than an impressive first book. The real problem comes after the third book. Then the reviews begin: 'Her first novel was terrific, but now, after two weak efforts in a row, it's becoming increasingly likely that its virtues were only an aberration.'"

I've noticed that the first books are often praised for their freshness, their lack of self-consciousness. In my case, "lack of consciousness" may have had something to do with it. And here I am referring not to what I know or don't know about the craft of writing but to what I didn't know about publishing. While I was writing my first book, I still believed that "PW" referred only to the accounting firm of Price Waterhouse, and not to the trade magazine *Publishers Weekly* as well. I did not know the importance of a "boxed review." I had never heard "blurb" used as a verb. When I was told my book was being sold to the "clubs," I thought that meant as in Med or Rotary. I guessed that first serial rights were a writer's adjunct to the First Amendment. I am serious. Ask my editor.

And then the reviews started to come in. They surprised me, every one of them. I read reviews that praised me as having skills that I never knew I had—related to my unusual use of structure and the simplicity of my prose. And I read the critical ones as well, which pointed out faults that I also never knew I had—related to my unusual use of structure and the simplicity of my prose. And then I read one, which I cannot quote exactly, since I threw it away, that said something to this effect: "It will be hard, if not impossible, for Amy Tan to follow her own act." Shortly after that, I broke out with hives.

I should explain that I have never been a particularly nervous person or someone prone to psychosomatic illnesses. But while writing the Second Book, I developed literal symptoms of the imagined weight of my task. Each morning, when I was not on the road doing promotion for my first book, I would dutifully sit at my desk, turn on my computer, and stare at the blank screen. And sure enough, my imagination would take off unbidden, unrestrained. And I would imagine hundreds, thousands of people looking over my shoulder, offering helpful suggestions:

"Don't make it too commercial."

"Don't disappoint the readers you've already won over."

"Make sure it doesn't look like a sequel."

"But what about Updike? What about stories that multiply like Rabbit's?"

"Seriously, what are the themes that will shape your oeuvre?"

"What's an oeuvre?"

"Forget oeuvre. Don't even think about themes."

"Just don't make it exotic. That's too obvious."

"Just make sure that men are portrayed in positive roles this time."

"No, no, if you think about political correctness, you're dead."

"Think about sources of inspiration."

"*Don't* think about the advance."

"*Don't* think about how much every single word on this page is worth."

"Don't think."

With all these imaginary people weighing me down, I developed a pain in my neck, which later radiated to my jaw, resulting in constant gnashing, then two cracked teeth, and a huge dental bill. The pain then migrated down my back, making it difficult for me to sit up straight during the long hours necessary for writing a Second Book. And while I was struggling to sit in my chair, with hot packs wrapped around my waist, I did not write fiction: I wrote speeches—thirty, forty, fifty of them, all about the old book, a book that was rapidly becoming the source of my irritations.

And when I was not writing speeches, I was giving them. And when I was not giving speeches, I was answering telephone calls or responding to letters asking me to appear at a fund-raiser, to give a talk at a university, to blurb the book of a first-time novelist, to judge a writing contest, to donate money to a worthy cause, to teach at a creative-writing workshop, to serve on a panel on the Asian-American experience, to write an introduction to someone's book, and so on and so forth. For a while, I averaged a dozen requests a day. For a while, I tried to answer them all. I said yes to many. But I also said no to many: No to being a judge for the Miss Universe contest. No to posing for a Gap ad. Thanks but no thanks to the five or six people who offered to let me write their complete life stories, fifty-fifty on the royalties since I was already a proven author. And when I found that I still had no time to write, that fully nine months out of the past year had been spent on the road and in strange hotel rooms, that I had no more than three consecutive days at any given time to write fiction, I started to say no to all of the requests. I wrote long, guilt-ridden letters of apology. And when I had written about a book's worth of apologies, I moved and changed my phone number.

In between my bouts of back pain, jet lag, and guilt, I did start writing my Second Book, or rather, my second *books*. For example, I wrote eighty-eight pages of a book about the daughter of a scholar in China who accidentally kills a magistrate with a potion touted to be the elixir of immortality. I wrote fifty-six pages of a book about a Chinese girl orphaned during the San Francisco earthquake of 1906. I wrote ninety-five pages about a girl who lives in northeast China during the 1930s with her missionary parents. I wrote forty-five pages about using English to revive the dead Manchu language and the world it described on the plains of Mongolia. I wrote thirty pages about a woman disguised as a man who becomes a sidewalk scribe to the illiterate workers of San Francisco's Chinatown at the turn of the twentieth century.

By my rough estimation, the outtakes must now number close to a thousand pages. Yet I don't look on those pages as failed stories. I see them as my own personal version of cautionary tales—what can happen if I *do* watch out, what can go wrong if I write as the author everyone thought I had become and not as the writer I truly was. What I found myself writing was a Second Book based on what I thought various people wanted—something fairy tale–like, or exotic, or cerebral, or cultural, or historical, or poetic, or simple, or complex. Simultaneously, I found myself writing the imagined review that the book was clichéd, sentimental, contrived, didactic, pedantic, predictable, and—worst of all, for the literary writer—a saga, perfect for a miniseries.

Perhaps these stories would have, or should have, died of their own accord before they could have reached their own happy or unhappy ending. But some of the stories could have been saved, the weedy bits trimmed away, as with any writing, until the true seed could be found, then taken as the core of the real book. It could have been a single image, part of a character, an imagined sound.

But those books were not meant to become anything more than a lesson to me on what it takes to write fiction: persistence imposed by a limited focus. The focus of a pool player, who sees none of the posturing of the opponent, only the trajectory of the object ball to its pocket. The focus required of a priest, a nun, a convict serving a life's sentence.

What I am talking about is idealistic, of course—to think that any writer could really ignore praise, criticism, phone calls, dinner invitations, let alone a spot on the rug, a spice rack in need of alphabetical organization. All these things demand attention.

So what I did was more mundane. I let the answering machine take my calls. I put on earphones and listened to the same music day in and day out to obliterate my censoring voice. And I wrote with persistence, telling myself that no matter how bad the story was, I should simply go on like a rat in a maze, turning the corner when I arrived there. And so I started to write another story, about a woman who was cleaning a house, the messy house I thought I should be cleaning. After thirty pages, the house was tidy, and I had found a character I liked. I abandoned all the pages about the tidy house. I kept the character and took her along with me to another house. I wrote and then rewrote, six times, another thirty pages, and found a question in her heart. I abandoned the pages and kept the question and put that in my heart. I wrote and rewrote one hundred fifty pages and then found myself at a crisis point. The woman had turned sour on me. Her story sounded like one long complaint. I felt sick for about a week. I couldn't write. I felt like the rat who had taken the wrong turn at the beginning and had scrambled all this way only to reach a dead end. It appeared that my strategy simply to plow ahead was ill-fated.

Who knows where inspiration comes from? Perhaps it arises from desperation. Perhaps it comes from the flukes of the universe, the kindness of muses. Whatever the case, one day I found myself asking, "But *why* is she telling the story?" And she answered back, "Of course I'm crabby! I'm talking, talking, talking, no one to talk to. Who's listening?" And I realized: A story should be a gift. She needs to *give* her story to someone. And with that answer, I was no longer bumping my nose against a dead-end maze. I leapt over the wall and on the other side mustered enough emotional force to pull me through to the end.

So what I have written finally is a story told by a mother to her daughter, now called *The Kitchen God's Wife*. I know there are those who will say, "Oh, a mother-daughter story, just like *The Joy Luck Club*." I happen to think the new book is quite different from the old. But yes, there is a mother, there is a daughter. That's what found me, even as I tried to run away from it.

I wish I could say that was the end of writing my Second Book, that I found my inspiration, and the rest was clickety-clack on the keyboard. But no, that happens only in fiction. In real life, I had hundreds of moments of self-doubt. I deleted hundreds of pages from my computer's memory. And one incident made me laugh out loud. When I was still some two hundred pages from finishing the book, a friend called with my first "review." It turned out that a woman in a book club in Columbus, Ohio, had stood up at the end of a discussion on *The Joy Luck Club* and announced with great authority: "Well, I just read Amy Tan's second book, and believe me, it's not *nearly* as good as the first!"

I still wonder what book the woman in Ohio read. Was this indeed proof of the apocryphal tale of publishing that puts fear in every writer's heart—that you're doomed to fail before you even start? No matter, because I would be the first to agree with the woman in Columbus. My second book was awful. After all, even I couldn't bear to finish it—that tale about the elixir of immortality. And the third book—about the orphan girl who becomes a con artist—that wasn't very good either. Thumbs down also on my fourth, fifth, sixth, and seventh books. But the eighth book—eight is always a lucky number—the eighth book is *The Kitchen God's Wife*. And regardless of what others may think, it is my favorite.

How could it not be? I had to fight for every single character, every image, every word. And the story is, in fact, about a woman who does the same thing: she fights to believe in herself. She does battle with myths and superstitions and assumptions—then casts off the fates that accompany them. She doesn't measure herself by other people's opinions. "What use?" she says. "Then you are always falling, falling, falling, never strong enough to stand up by yourself and go your own way." She is no innocent. She sees her fears, but she no longer lets them chase her.

And sometimes, in secret, she lets her imagination run wild with hope. She would not mind, not really, if someone came up to her at a literary luncheon and said, "How does it feel to have written your best book second?"

—*1992*

Afterword

by Oakley Hall

In the late 1960s, Blair Fuller and I met in Squaw Valley. We were both residents, we were both writers, we had both taught writing. I was director of the Programs in Writing at the University of California, Irvine, and Blair had taught at California State University, Hayward, and at Stanford University. Moreover he was a contributing editor to the *Paris Review* and knew a great many high-profile writers, such as George Plimpton and Peter Matthiessen. He also had family connections to Harper & Row. I had served on the staff of a writers' conference at Antioch College and had seen possibilities for one on the West Coast. At that time there were no such conferences in the West, nor regular ones elsewhere except for Bread Loaf, which had a lot of elitist minuses, such as staff and participants not being allowed to mingle.

At that time, West Coast writers rarely saw their agents and editors without expensive trips to New York. Blair and Diana Fuller and Barbara Hall and I had many happy cocktail hours discussing a conference in Squaw Valley that would rectify this. We knew John Buchman, manager of the Squaw Valley Ski Corporation, which had many empty spaces to offer in the off-season. It seemed to us that we could mount a conference featuring workshops, panels, talks, and readings, with agents and editors on hand, and parties and tennis as a major part of the week. All of us played tennis, and our experience had been that many editors and agents did also. We were aware that the conference ought to include participants whose tuitions would pay our costs.

These happy chats on the conference continued for a year or so. We also discussed these possibilities with writer friends in San Francisco, all of whom were enthusiastic.

Nothing happened in the way of progress, however, until one summer when Blair was on a Fulbright in Algeria, and I was lying in a bathtub in Squaw. Our friend Edwina Evers, partner with Blair in a bookstore in San Francisco, phoned to say she had spoken to someone of authority at the University of California Extension, and UC was willing to finance a first shot at a conference, if we would commit to putting it together. I did not have Blair to consult with, I was lying in the bathtub, and my thoughts ran to "Let this cup pass from me."

I committed.

So, in 1968 we proceeded to a trial year. I forget who the agents and editors were. Staff members were pals from San Francisco and elsewhere: Herb Gold, Barnaby Conrad, Jack Leggett, Bill Eastlake. I phoned Mark Strand to see if he would come. "Sure, I'll be your poet!" he said. We named ourselves the "Community of Writers," because this was the 1960s and *community* was an in-word.

My young daughter Brett and her friend Kate Klaussen would make sandwiches. Barbara Hall handled the office. John Buchman and the Ski Corporation provided workshop and meeting spaces. Parties were planned. A number of my students from UC Irvine showed up, to attend workshops and sleep on our roof. Richard Ford and wife Kristina inhabited a tent we erected on the front porch, and one night someone unspecified came out and peed on the tent. Sandwiches were provided at minimal prices with maximal kitchen mess. The nice UC Extension lady was very hands-on and tried to collect money from neighbors who showed up for lectures and panels. She was eventually to elope with Bill Eastlake.

Would we try it a second time? You bet; it had been fun, parties, tennis, good company! UC Extension, which is supposed to break even on its projects, had not quite done so, but came close. Blair and I would finance it out of our own pockets the second year.

David Perlman, a *San Francisco Chronicle* writer and science editor, also had a ski cabin in the valley. We persuaded him to head a nonfiction segment. Blair recruited illustrious writer and editor friends from New York. Our staff was impressive!

Also, what ho! Participant Kathryn Marshall found a publisher—Cass Canfield, from Harper and Row—for her novel that summer at the Community. And in one of those early years came Anne Rice with a conventional story to workshop, and additional material on a novel concerned with vampires. She left with an agent, a publisher, and maybe already a huge contract, and never looked back.

We applied for grants and set up a Playwrights Program, in an informal connection with the Actors' Studio in San Francisco, with the likes of Paul Blake, Ed Hastings, and John Lyon to direct productions. Those early summers we were running eight or ten fiction and poetry workshops; a playwrights' workshop, with three or four dramatized readings of the plays for the participants to attend; and a tennis tournament, the International Writers Doubles Championships, with junker typewriters sprayed gold for prizes.

Bill Evers did the legal work for us to become a non-profit corporation.

We began to realize that we were actually assisting young writers to become authors, exposing them to agents and editors who were always on the lookout for talented beginners just like those we attracted. We were having successes! Little by little, what had been an all-fun week became serious. We didn't have as many parties, and the tennis tournament had to be jettisoned, but the successes of our participants were very gratifying.

Amy Tan came, and was advised by an agent to turn a series of short stories about her mother's friends into a novel called *The Joy Luck Club*. She has been looking back ever since, as a generous supporter of the Community. Brett and Kate continued to make sandwiches.

The grants ran out and there was no way we could continue the Playwrights Program paying Equity scale to the actors, so we had to abandon it. Meanwhile a conference-on-the-conference was held, establishing a tradition that staff and participants eat and drink together. Screenwriters Gill Dennis and Tom Rickman devised our increasingly successful Screenwriters Program.

One of those first years Mainline, a huge Australian construction company, descended on the valley to buy up everything left over from the 1960 Winter Olympics that the Ski Corporation did not have tied down, and promptly went bankrupt because of labor fracases in Australia. The company's holdings in the valley thus came up for sale at bargain prices. Blair Fuller,

Burnett Miller, and I put our heads and money together to purchase the Nevada Center, a huge double A-frame structure of some thousands of square feet, which would house the conference summers and could be rented out in-season in various lucrative ways. We paid $85,000. Each of us thinks the purchase of the Nevada Center was his brilliant idea. Drunk with possibilities, we thought of our acquisition as an opera house, and, in July 1984, we actually managed to mount an opera, *The Mother of Us All,* by Virgil Thomson and Gertrude Stein. The aged and crotchety composer was on hand for rehearsals, shouting at the soprano: "Stop acting and sing!"

Blair was the hero of operating the building until it became financially viable, through thicks and thins of daunting proportions. The building was ultimately sold at a handsome profit to the Squaw Valley Ski Corporation. The interest from this transaction now pays the Community's year-round executive director.

William Fox retired as director of poetry, and Galway Kinnell and Sharon Olds came up with a program in which both participants and staff write and present a poem each day in workshop. The Poetry Program is so popular that an elaborate system of raffles and drawings had to be devised to make sure everyone talented enough to be admitted can be. Other programs have come in under the Community's umbrella. The Art of the Wild, directed by Jack Hicks, moved on to Yosemite after five years in Squaw. Writing the Medical Experience, doctors and patients in conference, directed by David Watts, MD, moved to Sarah Lawrence College after a summer at Squaw.

Years and decades whistled past. Brett Hall Jones, who as a child made sandwiches for the participants, is now the executive director. Kate Klaussen is the housing director. Galway Kinnell retired after directing the Poetry Program for seventeen years, replaced by Robert Hass. Louis Jones and Lisa Alvarez, former participants, replaced Carolyn Doty, who directed the Fiction Program for twenty years. Michael Carlisle directs nonfiction; Diana Fuller the Screenwriters Program. I am the emeritus general director; Blair Fuller is a director, as are longtime staff members James Houston, Richard Ford, Amy Tan, Joanne Meschery, Al Young, and Alan Cheuse.

It is impossible to list the writers and staff who have appeared on our brochures without leaving someone out. Many writers currently publishing have had a session, or more than one, at the Community. Many former participants have returned as staff. Each year we feature readings by former participants who have been published that year. More time for more of them is always needed. The Community publishes an online newsletter chronicling the publishing and other successes of its participants. We have become a community indeed.

Applicants for these programs hail from all over the United States and from foreign countries. About two-thirds of them request aid. Thanks mainly to the efforts of Barbara Hall and Diana Fuller, we have aid to give.

Other conferences have sprung from this one. Barnaby Conrad left Squaw to inaugurate the Santa Barbara Writers Conference, still in operation, and Jack Leggett the Napa Valley Conference, ditto. James B. Hall produced the Santa Cruz Conference for a year or two, and Leonard Michaels one at Berkeley.

The Community of Writers celebrates its thirty-ninth year in 2007.

AUTHOR BIOGRAPHIES

MAX BYRD was born in Atlanta, Georgia. He is the author of a number of detective novels, including *California Thriller*, which won the Shamus Award, and of the historical novels *Jefferson*, *Jackson*, and *Grant*. His most recent novel, *Shooting the Sun*, was published by Bantam in 2004. After teaching at Yale University and Stanford University, he joined the English Department at UC Davis. Now retired, he lives in Davis, California.

MICHAEL CHABON was born in Washington, D.C., and grew up in Columbia, Maryland. He is the author of two short story collections and several novels, including *The Mysteries of Pittsburgh*, *Wonder Boys*, and *The Amazing Adventures of Kavalier & Clay*, which was awarded the Pulitzer Prize for fiction in 2001. His most recent novel is *The Yiddish Policemen's Union*. He lives in Berkeley.

ALAN CHEUSE was born and raised in Perth Amboy, New Jersey. He is the author of three novels, including *The Grandmothers' Club* and *The Light Possessed*; three collections of short fiction; and several nonfiction books, including

Listening to the Page. His most recent work of fiction is *The Fires*. As a book commentator, he is a regular contributor to National Public Radio's *All Things Considered*. He teaches at George Mason University, and divides his time between Washington, D.C., and Santa Cruz, California.

MARK CHILDRESS was born in Monroe, Alabama, and grew up in Ohio, Indiana, Mississippi, and Louisiana. He is the author of the novels *A World Made of Fire*, *V for Victor*, *Tender*, *Crazy in Alabama*, and *Gone for Good*. He wrote the screenplay for the Columbia Pictures film of *Crazy in Alabama*, released in 1999. He has published three books for children, including *One Mississippi,* published in 2006 by Little, Brown. He lives in New York City.

JANET FITCH was born and grew up in Los Angeles. She is the author of the novel *White Oleander*, which has been translated into twenty-six languages. Her short stories have appeared in such journals as *Room of One's Own*, *Black Warrior Review*, and *Speakeasy*. Fitch teaches fiction writing in the Masters of Professional Writing program at the University of Southern California. Her most recent novel, *Paint It Black*, was published in September 2006 by Little, Brown. She continues to live in Los Angeles.

RICHARD FORD was born in Jackson, Mississippi. He is the author of three collections of stories and six novels, including *The Lay of the Land*, published in October 2006 by Knopf. He is editor of *The Granta Book of the American Short Story* (volumes one and two), and *The Granta Book of the American Long Story*. He is a member of the American Academy of Arts and Letters, and winner of a Pulitzer Prize for fiction and of a PEN/Malamud Award for Excellence in the Short Story. He lives in Maine.

LYNN FREED was born in Durban, South Africa. She is the author of seven books—*Reading, Writing, and Leaving Home: Life on the Page* (essays); *The Curse of the Appropriate Man* (stories); and the novels *House of Women, The Mirror, The Bungalow, Home Ground,* and *Friends of the Family.* She is the recipient of the inaugural Katherine Anne Porter Award from the American Academy of Arts and Letters, and has received fellowships, grants, and support from the National Endowment for the Arts and the Guggenheim Foundation. She lives in Northern California and teaches at UC Davis.

OAKLEY HALL was born in San Diego, California, and grew up in San Diego and Hawaii. He is the author of fourteen novels, eleven mystery novels, and two books on the writing process. Two of his novels have been made into major motion pictures, and his *Warlock* has been republished in the *New York Review of Books* Classics series. A new novel, *Love and War in California,* was published in 2007 by Thomas Dunne Books. He was director of the Programs in Writing at UC Irvine for twenty years. In 2004, he was awarded the *Poets and Writers Magazine* Writers For Writers Award. He makes his home in San Francisco and Squaw Valley.

SANDS HALL was born in Del Mar, California, and grew up in Squaw Valley. She is the author of the novel *Catching Heaven*, a Random House Reader's Circle selection and a Willa Award Finalist for Best Contemporary Fiction. Her produced plays include an adaptation of Alcott's *Little*

Women and the comedic drama *Fair Use.* Her book *Tools of the Writer's Craft,* was published by Moving Finger Press in 2005. In addition to the Squaw Valley Community of Writers, she teaches at conferences such as the Iowa Summer Writing Festival, and at UC Davis Extension Programs. She is an affiliate artist with the Foothill Theatre Company and lives in Nevada City.

JAMES D. HOUSTON was born in San Francisco, California, and grew up in the Bay Area. He has published twenty works of fiction and nonfiction, including the novels *Snow Mountain Passage, Continental Drift,* and *The Last Paradise,* which received an American Book Award. He has taught at Stanford University and UC Santa Cruz, among other institutions. In spring 2006, he held the Lurie Chair as distinguished visiting professor in Creative Writing at San Jose State University. His most recent novel, *Bird of Another Heaven,* was published in 2007 by Knopf. He lives in Santa Cruz, California.

DIANE JOHNSON was born in Moline, Illinois. She is the author of many works of fiction and nonfiction, including the trilogy *Le Mariage, Le Divorce,* and *L'Affaire.* She is a two-time finalist for both the Pulitzer Prize and the National Book Award. She makes her home in San Francisco and Paris.

LOUIS B. JONES was born in Chicago and grew up in Wilmette, Illinois. He is the author of the novels *Ordinary Money, Particles and Luck,* and *California's Over,* all three *New York Times* Notable Books. He is a National Endowment for the Arts fellow. He lives in the Sierra Nevadas.

ANNE LAMOTT was born in San Francisco and grew up in Northern California. She is the author of six novels, including *Hard Laughter, Rosie, Joe Jones, All New People,* and *Crooked Little Heart* (the sequel to *Rosie*), as well as four best-selling books of nonfiction—*Operating Instructions, Bird by Bird: Some Instructions on Writing and Life, Traveling Mercies,* and *Plan B: Further Thoughts on Faith.* Lamott has been honored with a Guggenheim Fellowship and has taught at UC Davis, as well as at writing conferences across the country. Her latest essay collection is titled *Grace (Eventually): Thoughts on Faith.* She lives in Northern California.

JOANNE MESCHERY was born in Gorman, Texas, and grew up in Boston, Massachusetts; California; and Nevada. She is the author of *In a High Place; A Gentleman's Guide to the Frontier,* which was nominated for a PEN/Faulkner Award; and *Home and Away.* She teaches at San Diego State University and makes her home in Southern California.

SANDRA SCOFIELD was born in Wichita Falls, Texas. She is the author of seven novels and a memoir, *Occasions of Sin.* One of her novels was a finalist for a 1991 National Book Award, and several have been included in the *New York Times Book Review*'s list of best books of the year. Her craft book, *The Scene Book: A Primer for the Fiction Writer,* was published by Penguin Books in 2007. She lives in Montana.

ROBERT STONE was born in Brooklyn, New York. He is the author of several novels, including *A Hall of Mirrors,* winner of a William Faulkner Award for best first novel; *Dog Soldiers,* winner of a National Book Award; *A Flag for Sunrise;*

Children of Light; Outerbridge Reach; and *Damascus Gate.* Stone has received Guggenheim and National Endowment for the Humanities fellowships, a five-year Mildred and Harold Strauss Living Award, a John Dos Passos Prize for Literature, and an American Academy and Institute of Arts and Letters Award. He lives in New York City.

AMY TAN was born in Oakland, California. Her first novel, *The Joy Luck Club*, was nominated for a National Book Award and a National Book Critics Circle Award and was a recipient of a Commonwealth Gold Award. Her memoir, *The Opposite of Fate*, appeared in 2003, and her most recent novel, *Saving Fish from Drowning*, was published by Putnam in 2005. Her other novels are *The Hundred Secret Senses, The Kitchen God's Wife,* and *The Bonesetter's Daughter.* She lives in Northern California.

AL YOUNG was born in Ocean Springs, Mississippi, on the Gulf Coast near Biloxi, and grew up in the South and in Detroit. Young has taught poetry and fiction writing at Stanford, UC Berkeley, UC Santa Cruz, UC Davis, Foothill College, Colorado College, Rice University, University of Washington, University of Michigan, University of Arkansas, and San Jose State University. His honors include a PEN–Library of Congress Award for Short Fiction, a PEN–USA Award for Non-Fiction, and two American Book Awards. His books include *Who is Angelina?, Sitting Pretty,* and *Seduction by Light.* In 2005, he was appointed Poet Laureate of California. He lives in Berkeley.